Your most affectionate wife
Charlotte

For my wife
BETTY NICHOLAS

and my daughter
CHARLOTTE O'BRIEN HENEMAN

THE CHAPLAIN'S LADY

Life and Love at Fort Mackinac

by
EDWARD NICHOLAS

© 1987
Mackinac Island State Park Commission
Mackinac Island, Michigan
First Printing 5,000 copies
Second Printing 2,000 copies, soft cover
750 copies, hard cover

PREFACE

John and Charlotte O'Brien treasured the letters they received from each other. They tied them up with string in tight little bundles, sometimes marked 'From the beloved to me', or 'Letters of mine tied up by the beloved'. After they had died, their son Lyster O'Brien kept their papers. No matter how much he moved about in his lifelong career as a soldier, he always had them safely stored somewhere. In his last years, retired from the army, he lived at the home of his daughter, Charlotte O'Brien Nicholas, my mother. The boxes of his parents' letters and his own valued papers were put away in the attic.

I knew him in those days. An old man in his seventies, he had ample time to spend with his three-, four-, five-year-old grandson. To me he was never 'Grandfather' but always 'Colonel'. I can remember that he told me about the Indians who came in the summers to camp on the beaches of Mackinac Island and about how in the winters he and his brothers skated on the frozen straits.

In the years after his death his boxes of papers were shifted from one attic or storeroom to another, as the family moved. In time they became mine to keep, valued but unopened. Finally in 1985 I untied the bundled letters and read them. There I discovered living people who had been only names to me before. Events and emotions of a distant past became real again, the long-forgotten everyday life of Fort Mackinac in the 1840's and 1850's. A distant past, and yet I had touched it, for the years were spanned by our two lifetimes, Lyster's and mine.

From the papers that he had preserved I have formed this book. Its words are John's and Charlotte's more than my own. I have invented nothing, but only tried to arrange and interpret the writings that they left. Much is immediate and poignant, much is unknown. There are a thousand questions that I would ask the Colonel now if I could but which remain forever unanswered.

I wish to express my gratitude to members of the staff of the Mackinac Island State Park Commission for their friendly and generous help in this project. Phil Porter has provided me with material from the historical records of the Fort, with which his own researches have made him familiar. And I especially thank Dr. David A. Armour, who has taken charge of the design and production of this book. To my pictures of the O'Brien family and their mementos he has added the illustrations, chosen from the Commission's archives, that recreate the scenes amid which the O'Briens lived in their years at old Fort Mackinac.

Edward Nicholas
January 1987

The two lives that bridge the years: Col. Lyster O'Brien with his grandson, the author of the book. This picture was taken in the summer of 1911, when the Colonel was in his 75th year and I was 4½ years old.

THE CHAPLAIN'S LADY

Life and Love at Fort Mackinac

As the boat approaches Mackinac Island, white land-marks appear against the dark bluffs of the shore. The most conspicuous is the long façade of the Grand Hotel, standing haughtily aloof from the disorderly commercial village that crowds around the harbor. Built in 1887, the hotel is a symbol of the Island's heyday in the decades following the Civil War, when people of wealth and fashion congregated here in the cool summers. Their sumptuous cottages on the high viewpoints, their yachts in the harbor, made Mackinac an outpost of Victorian elegance in the northland.

Symbol of an earlier and rougher time is old Fort Mackinac on the bluff behind the village. Its white walls and stubby blockhouses overlook the shining straits whose commerce they guarded. Not yachts but Indian canoes landed on the beaches in those days, laden with furs from the beaver forests of Wisconsin. A crude population thronged the village, Indian, French, American; trappers, woodsmen, traders, soldiers.

Walk up the steep inclined path to the Fort and enter by the sallyport gate where the sentry used to stand. Before you within the enclosure of earthworks and palisades the level parade ground lies as the garrison left it nearly a century ago. On one side is a two-story barracks that housed a company of soldiers. Along the rim of the bluff are the officers' quarters, long low buildings, one of wood and one of stone. Opposite these, high on a mound at the rear of the Fort, stands a white house with a veranda across the front; it was once known as the "Hill Quarters" and provided apartments for two more officers. Before it is a flagpole where the Fort's colors still fly. Elsewhere about the enclosure are various utilitarian buildings, offices, storerooms, hospital, guardhouse and the like. Everything is in proper military order, as if waiting for the garrison's return. The State Park Commission has restored and maintains it all as a monument of the Island's history. The officers' rooms are refurnished with antique pieces in the style of the old days. The parlors, bedrooms, kitchens of the Stone Quarters and the Hill Quarters seem ready for their former tenants to enter again.

Who were these people who lived here, looked out these windows over the wide straits, walked on this veranda? What were their moods and thoughts, their sense of life, as the beautiful summers passed and the long ice-locked winters enclosed them?

Go out by the wagon gate at the rear of the Fort, cross the grassy meadow that was used as a drill field, and enter the woods beyond. Here a road runs through the trees, maple and beech, birch and cedar, second growth, but still the enduring northern forest that has always mantled the Island. Following the road deep into the woods, you come presently to a clearing enclosed by a white picket fence. This is the Post Cemetery. The wind seldom blows here in the shelter of the woods, and the flag above the soldiers' graves hangs limply. On level ground in front are military ranks of small tombstones, gray and identical, some inscribed with the names of the dead, some marked simply "Unknown". Once perhaps all were known, but the original wooden markers rotted as the years passed and half the names were lost.

Post Cemetery, Fort Mackinac. Charlotte O'Brien's grave is at the rear surrounded by chains.

On the rising slope toward the rear of the enclosure a few larger and more elaborate headstones mark the graves of officers. Among these, near one corner of the cemetery, stands a dignified marble obelisk, its tiny precinct guarded by an iron chain mounted on four low posts. On one face of the stone is carved, with capricious capitalization, "Under this Monument are Deposited the remains of CHARLOTTE Obrien BORN AT East Lockenge, Berkshire, ENGLAND SEPT. 12, 1812 who Departed this life March 17, 1855."

There must be a story behind the presence of this young Englishwoman here, her grave so signalized above the humble ranks of the soldier tombstones. What was the life that ended here on a winter day in 1855?

She died on the 17th of March, a Saturday. Her husband, the Rev. John O'Brien, the Chaplain of Fort Mackinac, was staggered by his loss, too bewildered to act. Unasked and with the utmost tact, the Commandant of the garrison, Major Thomas Williams, came forward and himself took charge of the funeral arrangements. He had a coffin made, had it lined with fine fabric and a silver plate affixed, engraved "Charlotte 17 March". On Monday, the day of the funeral, he had the corpse brought and placed in his own parlor in the Stone Quarters. The room was deeply robed in mourning. There were few flowers to be had, but a sorrowing friend, Mrs. Abbott, wreathed forget-me-nots with evergreen and ivy around the silver plate and placed on Charlotte's bosom geraniums cut from her house plants.

There was a severe snowstorm that day, fearfully cold. Major Williams had the flag of the Fort lowered to half staff and had the entire garrison turned out to march in formation. People from the village were struggling up the slippery way to the Fort. A procession formed, soldiers and villagers, and set out through the snow-filled woods toward the cemetery, toward the grave that Major Williams had ordered dug in the frozen ground. In spite of the storm it was the largest procession, John O'Brien thought, that had ever been assembled here. With him, trudging behind the coffin, were three little boys, his sons. They wrote letters about it later to their elder brother, Lyster, who was away at college. Twelve-year-old Noel wrote:

"We are very lonely sinse our dear Mother died, on Monday the day our dear Mother was buried it was very cold and it stormed very hard . . . Allan says that he did not think he would follow Mother to the grave so soon."

And Bertie, who was ten, said "It was very painful to see our dear Mother lowered in the grave. but it was god's will to take her from us this is all that I can say to you now."

"It was a sad and solemn scene", their father, the Chaplain, wrote, "and deeply impressed all — she was loved in life in death honor'd and respected . . . She rests in the tomb, but her spirit is in glory enjoying the light of her Saviours countenance." He felt much indebted to Major Williams for all that he had done; "that debt has been encreased from the delicate manner in which all was arranged — flowing as it did from an accomplished mind and a sympathising heart . . . were it for his own sister he could not offer a higher tribute of respect."

"I did what my heart devised," Major Williams told him, "but alas, how feeble an expression of my feelings. If I could soothe or console, I would; — there is but *one* source of consolation! But, my deep affliction attests my sympathy."

Gateway at Fort Mackinac through which Charlotte's body was taken for burial. Drawn in 1854 by Alfred R. Waud.

Charlotte O'Brien — a tintype made from an 1848 Daguerreotype.

Church at East Lockinge, Berkshire — Charlotte's parents were married in this ancient Anglican church; and her father, Thomas Tull, is said to have been buried under its floor. During Charlotte's first 18 years this church and its teachings formed her earnestly religious mind.

S uch was the sorrowful and early end of a life that had begun in gladness and well-being in the pleasant surroundings of an English village. East Lockinge is some twenty miles south of Oxford, lying in the valley of a brook that flows from the Berkshire downs into the Vale of the White Horse. Here in a pretty pastoral countryside Charlotte Tull spent a happy childhood. Her family was well-to-do, and even after her father died when she was six they continued to live in an abundant style. She and her older sister and two brothers were well educated. Charlotte went away to school, where she acquired the accomplishments proper for an English lady. She became familiar with literature and the arts, learned to draw well and to write well, studied music and played the piano. Her world of friends and relatives was wide; she traveled and visited all over southern England. What scanty records remain give us a glimpse of her with a group of high-spirited friends at Sandbach in Cheshire, playing parlor games, or staying with her best friend, Eliza Cooper, in Denbigh House near Ryde on the Isle of Wight.

What was young Charlotte like? There is no early picture of her, but a daguerreotype made years later shows a very pretty woman with long dark-brown straight hair that she parted in the middle, the darkest of brown eyes and a gentle mouth — a delicate, sensitive face, more thoughtful than merry. Of letters that she may have written in her girlhood only one remains, a blithe kid-sister note to her older brother, John Tull. She had copied two poems for him, "The Soldier's Tear" and "Sea Song", suitable masculine fare, she must have thought, for a man of 22.

"My dear John", she wrote below the poems, "It is written very badly, but the pen will not go and the knife will not cut and the paper is damp and the ink very thick and the Mama is calling and the table is jogging and the writer has got a fit of the scribbles — so no more at present from yours C. T."

Charlotte Tull's album

Edward Nicholas

What little is known of her at this period of her life is reflected from the pages of her Album. This is a blank-book, bound in red morocco leather impressed with gilt designs. On the spine in gilt is the word ALBUM and on the cover CHARLOTTE TULL. It is an elegant volume, expressive of the modest luxury in which the Tulls lived in those days. At home it probably lay on a table in the parlor, and when Charlotte traveled it went with her. In it she gathered her friends. From time to time and place to place they filled the pages with poems and pictures. These were talented young people. Their pencil drawings, some no larger than a playing card, were exquisite; they painted beautiful little watercolors of flowers, a peacock, girls in a landscape. Pictures and poems alike expressed the mood of the Romantic Age, the age of Keats and Shelley. Their themes were the beauty of nature, the transience of life, the mercies of God, all suffused with a gentle melancholy.

An example of Charlotte's own work, dated November 5, 1828 — she was sixteen — was entitled "Walthamstow Ferry Fishery". On the upper half of the page she drew a pencil sketch of a rustic bridge over a stream, two fishermen standing on it, trees and a house on the bank. Below she wrote this poem:

> Go where the water glideth gently ever,
>   Glideth by meadows that the greenest be —
> Go listen to our own beloved river,
>   And think of me
> Wander in forests where the small flower layeth
>   Its fairy gem beside the giant tree,
> Listen to the dim brook pining while it playeth,
>   And think of me!

Walthamstow Ferry Fishery

Go where the water glideth gently ever,
    Glideth by meadows that the greenest be—
Go listen to our own beloved river.
                And think of me
Wander in forests, where the small flower layeth
    The fairy gem beside the giant tree;
Listen to the dim brook pining while it playeth
                And think of me!

*Walthamstow Ferry Fishery — Signed C. T. Nov*r *3, 1828. Charlotte was 16 at this time. Walthamstow was a village just north of London, since engulfed by the spreading city.*

Charlotte's friends, enshrined in the Album and in her heart, made up her world. Her family affections were strong. She and her sister Caroline were "all in all to each other", and her brothers and mother hardly less so. Ironically, it was the trusting warmth and closeness of family affection among the Tulls that brought their comfortable life to ruin and caused them to emigrate to America.

Charlotte's elder sister, Caroline, fell in love with a wealthy widower, a London merchant twenty years older than she, one Mr. Browne. Mrs. Tull was much opposed to a marriage, because Caroline was so young and he so much older, but at last she reluctantly gave consent. Caroline and her husband lived in London "in very good style" for several years, and Mr. Browne seemed to be everything that the Tulls could wish him to be. Their natural response then, when he came to them and asked their help with some temporary business difficulties, was that Mrs. Tull and her sons generously loaned him large sums of money. Alas, the difficulties proved to be more than temporary; they were disaster. Mr. Browne's fortune vanished, and with it all the money that the Tulls had loaned him.

Their luxurious way of life was at an end and their fine house in East Lockinge must be sold. Charlotte, preparing to leave the familiar home and surroundings of her childhood, distilled her feelings into a sonnet, written in the Album:

> Adieu, beloved and lovely home! Adieu
>> Thou pleasant mansion and ye waters bright
> Ye walks, ye aged elms, ye shrubberies light
>> My own contemporary trees that grew
>>> E'en with my growth, ye flowers of orient hue
> A long farewell to all! Ere fair to sight
>> In summer shine ye bloom with beauty dight
> Your halls we leave for scenes untried and new.
>> Oh! shades endeared by memory's magic power
> With strange reluctance from your paths I roam!
>> But home lives not in walk or tree or flower
> Nor dwells tenacious in one only dome.
>> Where smiling friends adorn the social hour
> Where they, the dearest are, there will be home.

At age seventeen, and ever after, place meant much to Charlotte, but people more.

Oh! sweet is morn's first breeze that strays on the mountain,

And sighs o'er its bosom, and murmurs away;

And bright is the beam which upsprings from day's fountain,

And breaks o'er the East in its golden array!

And lovely the riv'let incessantly flowing,

Which winds gently murm'ring its course through the plain,

We welcome the beacon which faithfully glowing,

Cheers the heart of the mariner tossed on the main.

But sweeter, my God, is thy voice of compassion,

Which soft as the summer dew falls on the mind;

Which whispers the tidings of life and salvation,

And casts the dark shadows of sorrow behind.

Edward Nicholas

"Oh! sweet is morn's first breeze . . ." — The drawing, on an embossed card, is signed in the corner "Charlotte 1830 July 21st." The scene is probably imaginary.

Drawing of a castle — Signed C T June 23^d 1830. Untitled, and may be either an actual or imaginary place.

Edward Nicl

The Tull family moved to Bradley, a Hampshire village, where the two brothers, young men in their early 20's, tried to re-establish the family's life on the scale they had known before. After two years, discouraged, they decided to go to America to make a fresh start. Mrs. Tull and Charlotte were greatly urged by a wealthy relative to remain, but Mrs. Tull would not let her boys go without her, and Charlotte would not leave her mother. So the entire family, including Caroline and Mr. Browne, gathered together what means they had left and "with many sad thoughts and blinding tears" took ship for America. In Charlotte's Album, which she carried with her, was a farewell poem by Eliza Cooper:

> Alas, it is in vain that we would hide
> The winter of the heart . . .

They crossed in July, 1832. For a time in August they tarried in Rochester, New York, but then moved on and settled in a frontier village, Monroe, in Michigan Territory. Why they chose Monroe, or how they even heard of it, is not recorded. Perhaps the brothers understood that land was cheap and opportunities plentiful in the undeveloped West.

Monroe stood on the banks of the River Raisin where it flowed into Lake Erie, about fifty miles south of Detroit. All around lay flat land, marshy and covered with hardwood forest. The roads through the swamps and bogs were almost impassable for wheeled vehicles. In 1832, when the Tulls arrived, there were five or six hundred inhabitants. Just where or how the Tulls lived in this unkempt community is unknown, except that John Tull was later said to have been "a country gentleman" at this period. An English gentleman he surely was, but beyond that the term must have meant, not the leisurely management of an estate, but hard work as a farmer.

Charlotte was just twenty years old when she came to Monroe. She had come unwillingly, because the rest of them came. Not only was she heartbroken at parting from her friends in England, but her conscience told her that this expedition in search of material benefit was wrong. She, the "pious one of the family", could not consent to such worldly purposes; it was a "declension" from spiritual integrity. She expressed her homesickness in poetry. Of all the lost friends the "best and dearest" was Eliza Cooper. She wrote a poem "To my absent friend":

> Eliza, oh that I could press thee
> To my weary careworn heart
> Look on thy dear face, and press thee
> And never never from thee part . . .
>
> Oh! dost thou think of me, alone
> And severed far from mine own land
> Am I as once I was, thine own
> Thy cherished one? or is the band
>
> Of friendship broken? no, ah no
> Thou'rt true my dearest friend to me,
> This thought shall gild the lonely hours
> Till our blest time of meeting be.

Next to her friends she must have remembered most long-ingly the tiny ancient church at East Lockinge, in which her strong religious convictions had first been formed. In Monroe she found no Episcopal church, but only a din of hammering and sawing, a framework of raw lumber, where a church was being built at a corner of the village square.

By the time it was completed and opened for divine service on February 3, 1833, Charlotte had met its Rector, a young Irishman five or six years older than she, the Reverend John O'Brien. He was proud and excited with his carpenter-gothic edifice. He wrote enthusiastically to the Missionary Society that had sent him to this newly formed parish:

"The largest assemblies ever collected in the village attended the morning and evening services . . . The Church is a neat building, and accomodates between 300 and 400 persons, the body of the house 36 by 46 feet, exclusive of a vestry room in the rear."

He sent the Society a drawing of the church, showing its tower with little pinnacles which were "allowed by all to be exceedingly well proportioned, and present the first interesting object to persons entering our village . . . A subscription was lately circulated through the village for the purchase of a bell not less than 700 pounds . . . When we look back, and think what we were sixteen months ago, with a number scarcely sufficient to form a vestry — poor and of no repute — compelled to meet in a cold, uncomfortable room — we have much cause for gratitude to the bountiful giver of every good."

Charlotte was strongly attracted to the handsome young Irish preacher. His face was intellectual, with dark eyes gazing intensely, a sharp nose, tight lips and a high forehead from which wavy brown hair was combed back, clustering over his ears and his clerical collar. In due time he was asked to make his contribution to her Album. In that book of romantic and visionary poetry and pictures he wrote no poem, drew no picture. None of that gossamer stuff for John O'Brien. What he wrote was a short, zealous sermon:

" 'Always abounding in the work of the Lord.' The whole spirit of Christianity breathes activity, and arouses to industry . . . it demands the exertion of the whole man, the devotion of all times and seasons, the surrender of all we have, & all that we are, to the work of the Lord. And what is this work? It is unreserved obedience to the law of God . . ." He continued in this relentless vein for the rest of the page.

John O'Brien's drawing of Trinity Church, Monroe. Published in the April, 1833 **Missionary Record.**

MISSIONARY RECORD

OF THE

Domestic and Foreign Missionary Society,

OF THE PROT. EPIS. CHURCH IN THE UNITED STATES OF AMERICA.

EDITED BY THE SECRETARY.

| VOL. I. | APRIL, 1833. | No. 4. |

TRINITY CHURCH, MONROE, MICHIGAN TERRITORY.

Domestic Department.

MICHIGAN.

We have the satisfaction of placing before our readers, in the present number, a representation of the Church edifice at Monroe, Michigan Territory, erected under the auspices of the Domestic and Foreign Missionary Society.

In the summer of 1831, the Executive Committee appropriated a certain sum place, and on the 10th of December following, the Rev. John O'Brien began to discharge there the duties of his office. At that time there were but two decided Episcopalians belonging to the congregation. Now it consists of about two hundred and fifty, between twenty-five and thirty of whom are communicants.

From the report of the Rev. Mr. O'Brien officiating at Monroe.

"*March* 12*th.*—It will be gratifying to

John O'Brien

His passionate dogmatism pleased Charlotte rather than repelled her. She too had dedicated herself utterly to the Lord. When she was seventeen, still in England, she had written out and formally signed a long, emotional Covenant with God, which she kept with her ever after to remind her to live by its terms:

"Hear oh thou God of heaven, and record it in the book of thy remembrance, that henceforth I am thine, entirely thine . . . The whole frame of my nature, all the faculties of my mind, and all the members of my body, would I present this day before thee as a living sacrifice. In thy service I desire to spend all the remainder of my steps on earth . . ."

By more than the earnestness of their religious dedication these two young people were drawn to each other. They shared the manners and the memories, they spoke with the accent, of that Britain from which they were exiles. In the rude American village of Monroe, who else was there for either of them?

On March 2, 1836, they were married in John's own Trinity Church by their friend, the Reverend William Lyster.

Charlotte O'Brien's sketch of Trinity Episcopal Church, Monroe.

Edward Nicholas

Their honeymoon trip in the following summer, with the conventional destination of Niagara Falls, was a kind of ecclesiastical pilgrimage. For Charlotte it was a journey of delight, with John's friends of the clergy welcoming them along the way in their homes and churches, and with frequent services in which John assisted and sometimes preached — "a sermon of truth from my dear husband, every word of which went to my heart."

Their first child was born on December 7, 1836. They named him Lyster Miller O'Brien after two close friends. Charlotte was enchanted with him. In a letter dated August 18, 1838, to John who had gone to visit Bishop Biddle in Pennsylvania, she wrote ". . . baby is in so frolicsome a mood that he is ever jogging my elbow, and peeping up at me his merry little face so funnyly, that I cannot forebear to answer him with a tickle that drives him off only to return for another — dear little fellow! He goes twenty times a day to the door crying Papa, Papa . . . oh! how I wish that the time of your absence had expired! pray write to me, as soon as you receive this, & let it be a *long long letter* . . . May God bless you, my own dear husband in all you say & do, & wherever you go — & bring you home safe & well to your most affectionate little wife Charlotte O'Brien."

They lived in a one-story brown house on the bank of the River Raisin, which they called the Rectory but which the village knew as "The O'Brien Cottage". A porch across the front was enclosed by a trellis in which were three gothic-arched openings, the center one for the doorway. Charlotte drew a pencil sketch of it under which she wrote:

> 'Tis but an humble cot, yet there
>   Have peace and love a shrine,
> And oh! to this fond heart how dear,
>   For I may call it *mine.*
>
> May no rude hand this spot deform
>   No biting winds impair it
> And may the red wing of the storm
>   Pass ever by and spare it!

She bore a second son, Allan Henry, in August, 1839. With her two dear boys, her devoted husband and her gothic cottage, with new American friends she had made, the tenor of her life was set. She was happy. And yet — this wasn't England. Letters from relatives, letters and English newspapers that Eliza Cooper sent, kept reminding her of the idyllic life she had left behind. She was homesick sometimes. Her longing took form in a poem, "To E. C."

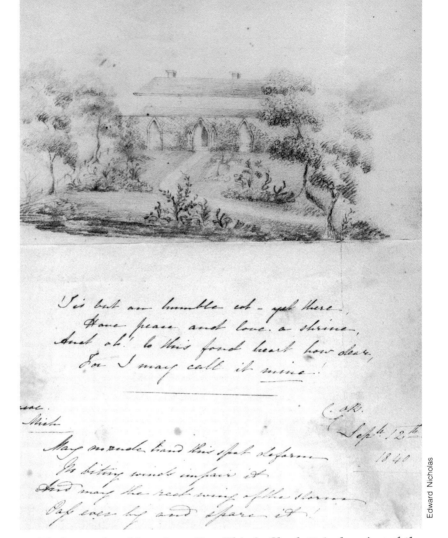

" 'Tis but an humble cot . . ." — *This is Charlotte's drawing of the house where she and John lived in Monroe. It stood on the bank of the River Raisin on a street still called O'Brien Street. This drawing is dated on Charlotte's 28th birthday. The second stanza of the poem, written in a different ink, seems to have been added later.*

No more my friend do I ramble with thee
 O'er the glittering sands by the dark blue sea
Nor into thine ear pour the hidden store
 Of my heart's cherished thoughts
  No more — no more

Oh for those days spent so sweetly with thee
 In thy sweet Ivied Cot by the glorious Sea
Too swiftly they flew. And in my hearts core
 Their records lie buried
  No more — no more

John O'Brien likewise was not long content with his small parish in Monroe. For Charlotte's sake, and by his own desire as well, he began to explore the chances of finding employment in England. One doubt in particular troubled him. When he had arrived in America he was in deacon's orders only, and was not ordained a minister until after he came to Monroe. Would this ordination be recognized in England? He wrote with this question to a boyhood chum, James Wright, who had also entered the ministry and had a church in Cheshire. The two of them had been boys together in Kilkenny, a town southwest of Dublin in Ireland. James had lived there in a stately home, Foulksrath Castle, which his father leased from the Earl of Portarlington. That "dear old spike of a castle", James called it. John's letter stirred him to memories of "the happy moments we have spent together — many of them might have been better spent — yet I look back to them with feelings of a pleasing character which many other portions of my life cannot afford me."

He forwarded John's letter to the Bishop of Chester, and sent John a transcript of his Lordship's reply.

"London April 29. My dear Mr. Wright, I am sorry your valuable correspondent is precluded from that which he so naturally desires and prefers, the opportunity of exercising his ministry in this country . . . a particular Act of Parliament 26 Geo. III c. 84 prohibits altogether from officiating 'in his Majesty's dominions' those who have been ordained by the bishops of the United States. I suppose that this law had its origin in a dread of republican views, which we need not now apprehend: still the law remains, and is an absolute barrier. I regret that Mr. O'Brien was not aware of this, because it probably would have influenced him in respect of his ordination . . . I am, my dear sir, very faithfully yours, J. B. Chester."

John did not give up easily. He hoped that the Bishop of Chester could be persuaded to bring up a bill in the House of Lords to repeal the obnoxious Act, and to this end he corresponded urgently with James Wright and others who might have influence. To no avail. "I can feel for you, my dear brother," Wright wrote to him, "separated from all that is dear to you in this world, and tied as you are by circumstance to a foreign soil."

Why John had emigrated to America before he was ordained is obscure. Indeed, almost nothing is known of his early life except that he had acquired an excellent classical education, probably at Trinity College in Dublin, was fluent in Latin and well-read in English literature and exegesis of Scripture. He left college in 1827 and came to America soon after. A vague tradition has lingered among his descendants that political activities or associations made it advisable for him to leave abruptly when he did.

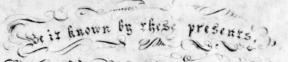

Be it known by these presents,

That we, CHARLES P. McILVAINE, D.D. Bishop of the Protestant Episcopal Church, in the diocese of Ohio; holding, under the protection of Almighty God, an ordination at Gambier, on the seventh day of September, in the year of our Lord, one thousand eight hundred and thirty three; did admit our well beloved in Christ, the Reverend John O'Brien (of whose good morals, competent learning and sound faith and knowledge of the holy scriptures, we were well assured) into the holy order of Priest in the Church of Christ; and him the said Reverend John O'Brien did then and there rightly and canonically ordain Priest, according to the form and manner prescribed and used by the Protestant Episcopal Church in the United States of America.

In testimony whereof we have hereunto set our hand and seal, the day and year above written.

Chas. P. McIlvaine.

This is John O'Brien's ordination by an American bishop, which stood as a barrier to his ever returning to Great Britain to practice his ministry.

In any case, the door was closed against return. He must remain, and Charlotte with him, American for life. To make the best of that necessity, he began to cast about for some new post that would provide a better living than his meager stipend at Monroe. He attended Conventions of the clergy, sought the company of bishops and often visited his influential friends in Detroit. In that city he met important people, among them Michigan's foremost citizen, Gen. Lewis Cass, who had been Governor of the Territory and Secretary of War and was later a candidate for the Presidency. Probably through the influence of Gen. Cass, John was offered a military appointment as United States Army Chaplain at Fort Mackinac.

In this post he would receive a Captain's pay of $40 a month — more than twice what his parish paid — a Captain's quarters, rations for his family of four, wood fuel for his stoves, medicines and sundry other perquisites. It was an inviting prospect; he accepted it.

On the ninth of May in 1842 he conducted services for the last time in Trinity Church in Monroe and made his farewell address to the congregation. Navigation on Lake Huron was resuming as the ice that had locked the straits broke up. With all their possessions the O'Briens embarked at Detroit on a steamboat bound for their new home in the North.

United States, Island of Mackinaw, October 1842

Three drawings by Col. Henry F. Ainslie of Mackinac Island in 1842, the year the O'Briens arrived.

Mackinac Island in the 1840's was becalmed in a slack time between its two eras of glory. The heroic days of the fur trade were over, and though the Indians still converged on the island every summer in fleets of canoes, they no longer brought cargoes of furs, for they had depleted the beaver in Wisconsin. The Chippewa had become pensioners. They camped in long lines of tepees on the beaches around the harbor and waited for the annual "Indian payment", when the government would distribute, in accordance with treaty, their tribute of blankets, cloth, guns, utensils and ornaments. The village now made a prosaic living from the fish industry, processing, salting, packing and shipping whitefish and lake trout. Summer visitors were arriving on the steamboats to stay in the bleak boxy little hotels by the waterfront, but they were few and the days were still decades away when vacationers by the thousands would throng the Island with excitement and gaiety. Fort Mackinac in the 40's still housed its company of soldiers, unconcerned now about hostile Indians or a British landing and stalled in a peacetime routine of drill, training and ceremony.

United States Mackinaw Island & Fort, Chippeway Indians travelling, taken from the Steamer 1845

United States, Fort & village of Michilimackinac, State of Michigan. Chippeway Indians encamped to receive their Annual presents Sept 18.

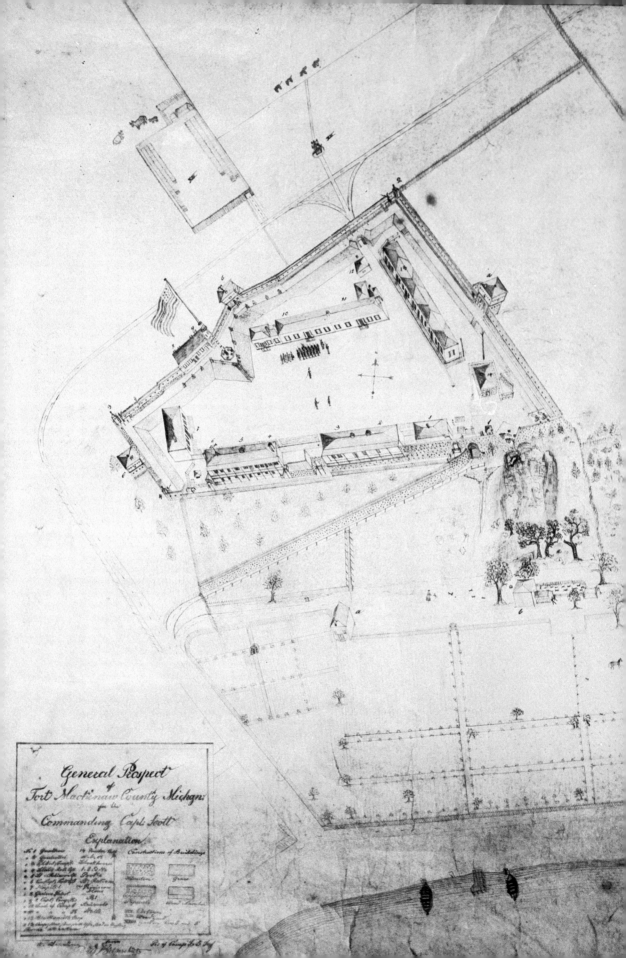

General Prospect
of
Fort Mackinaw County Michgn:
for the
Commanding Capt. Scott

Explanation

The South Sally ramp at Fort Mackinac. The Hill Quarters is in the upper right.

The house, called the Hill Quarters, into which the O'Briens moved was the newest one in the Fort, having been built only seven years before. It contained two separate apartments, of which the O'Briens probably occupied the one on the western end, while various officers successively were their neighbors on the east. On the ground floor the O'Briens had a front parlor with a bay window, a master bedroom for John and Charlotte, a smaller room they used as a study, and toward the back a dining room, kitchen and pantry. Up stairs in the half-story under the pitched roof were several small bedrooms where the children slept and a housemaid when they had one. Underneath was a cellar for storage, and in front a veranda ran the length of the house. Standing on the highest point of the Fort, it overlooked the parade ground, the officers' quarters and the parapets and gun platforms on the rim of the bluff. The jumble of the village was far below, where fine white houses mingled with unpainted shacks and warehouses, and piers jutted into the harbor to receive the steamboats and sailboats that came and went. Beyond and above lay the wide lake and the sky, so that the house seemed enveloped in spaciousness and freedom. It was a delightful place to live.

Fort Mackinac drawn in 1842 by Private W. Brenschutz

Before the Rev. Mr. O'Brien came, the Fort had never had a Chaplain or a chapel, but for him Captain Martin Scott provided a room in one of the Fort's buildings, where a pulpit and other furnishings were installed. Here John O'Brien stood, an imposing figure in his black clerical robes, on Sunday morning, June 19, 1842. In rows on the benches before him the soldiers of the garrison sat, decorously dressed in their uniform coats and wearing their side arms. They had turned out at the summons of a bugle call, assembled in formation on the parade ground and marched into the chapel for the service. A number of people from the village below had also walked up to join the congregation.

Presently Mr. O'Brien launched his sermon. "Salvation! What a word!" he exclaimed, and went on to chide them for caring too little for that word. "With apathy and indifference have you listened to the wondrous scheme of redemption." It was afflicting and awful, he told them, to see men eagerly gratifying their appetites and passions, pursuing honor and ambition, but closing their ears against the word whereby they might be saved. "Man is a sinner and without salvation must perish. You may be too proud to acknowledge this . . . too much occupied with the world's business or pleasure." Sitting silent before him, the congregation could not answer these charges, so the preacher pleaded their defense for them, — and then demolished it. "Oh, you will say, I never did anyone any harm, I was always inoffensive and gentle in my conduct, . . . I have been a kind parent, an affectionate husband, a faithful friend . . . my character is without a stain, my reputation without a blemish. But that is not the question. Hast thou loved the Lord thy God, hast thou loved him supremely, hast thou loved him continually from the first dawning of reason to the present moment? . . . Have you never loved the creature more than the Creator, the world more than God, pleasure more than Him?" Yes, they were sinners, all sinners, and had transgressed the law of God.

This sermon was one that Mr. O'Brien had delivered a number of times before, in Monroe, Detroit and elsewhere. It was more harsh than most of his sermons. He may have thought that these soldiers were probably a hard lot, and that severe chastisement was needed to get their attention.

His voice rose now to an oratorical climax as he promulgated the divine wrath they had incurred. "The law you have broken rolls over you its dread anathema and utters its tremendous curse . . . Before you is the great white throne, and Him that sits on it, from whose face the heavens and the earth flee away, and there is no place found for them, and there are the flaming records, and there are the accusing spirits and there are the ministers of vengeance and the avenger of blood is at your heels! . . . What will you do to be saved?" Then the preacher moderated his tone. He now addressed the sinners before him as Brethren. "Brethren . . . take your bible,

The first two pages of one of John O'Brien's sermons.

Edward Nicholas

unfold its sacred pages. There and there alone can you find an . . . answer. Believe on the Lord Jesus Christ and thou shalt be saved." In the Bible and nowhere else, he declared, there is salvation, an everlasting salvation, perfect, sure and lasting. Salvation! "Oh, I would not have that word erased from the bible for ten thousand worlds. Let the sun be blotted out of the firmament of heaven and run riot thro' the universe of God, but let this word remain in this blessed book."

Again Mr. O'Brien invoked the wrath of God upon those who would neglect His mercy: "The Judge is at the door, the trumpet is sounding, the books are opening, the dead are rising . . . the rocks themselves rush to ruin, the elements are melting with fervent heat, all the universe of matter is but as fuel for the universe of fire . . . oh, whither will you fly?" And then, again relenting, he closed his sermon with words of hope. "Look to Christ and be saved, for he is your only refuge . . . he waiteth to be gracious, and stretches out his arm to receive you, to bid you welcome."

The earliest photograph of the inside of Fort Mackinac. 1860's. The Hill Quarters is behind the flagpole.

When the service ended, the soldiers filed out, formed ranks on the parade ground and were dismissed. Whether or not they were convinced of their peril as sinners, or led to love Mr. O'Brien's terrifying God, their new Chaplain had let them know at the outset that the military discipline under which they lived would be matched henceforward by a spiritual discipline no less rigorous in its demands.

The arrival of a resident clergyman was a great event for the Protestants of the Island, who had had only occasional services by visiting ministers. John O'Brien undertook to serve the village as well as the garrison. He preached twice on Sundays, in the morning at the Fort, in the evening at the Old Mission Church or in the Court

Interior of the Old Mission Church where John preached in the evenings.

Detail of the Hill Quarters in 1842. The O'Briens lived on the left side of the building.

Room on the upper floor of the County Courthouse on Market Street. He taught a Sunday School, visited the sick and comforted the bereaved. He distributed Testaments and thousands of tracts. These efforts were beyond his obligation, for his duty was only to the Fort, but he devoted himself gladly to the needs that he found.

For Charlotte, establishing the comforts of home in her fine house so beautifully sited on its hill, this was at once a new life and a confirmation of exile. For it was certain now that she and John would never return to England. Through her mind must have run sometimes the refrain of the poem she had written for Eliza Cooper, that friend who personified for her all that she had left behind of her childhood and her native land. "No more — no more!"

She was pregnant again during the first summer and winter at the Fort. When her third son was born on January 19, 1843, she named him Noel Cooper — "Nony." Had he been a girl, he would surely have been Eliza Cooper O'Brien.

Just two years later the family was complete with the birth of yet another son, Herbert Leigh O'Brien — "Bertie."

Keeping house at Mackinac for this growing family was not easy. The Fort was isolated, the village small and poor. Household needs of every kind — clothes, shoes, utensils, lamps — were either high-priced or not available at all. Each year after winter's grip on the Island was released by the break-up of the ice about the first of May, and the steamboats began to call again, one or the other

View of Detroit in 1836 painted by William James Bennett.

of the O'Briens would go down the lake to Detroit for two or three weeks of shopping and visiting. The letters that passed between them during these times of separation are the principal record that remains to us of their lives in the Mackinac years.

In Detroit there were many hospitable friends with whom they used to stay. One was the Right Reverend Samuel A. McCoskry, the Episcopal Bishop of Michigan. Another was Charles C. Trowbridge, President of the Michigan State Bank, in whose "social mansion," Charlotte said, "there is everything to cheer the mind of the christian, by the beautiful union of wealth & beneficence, piety and talent." Trowbridge had been John's strongest friend and protector ever since the earliest Monroe days; at news that John was coming to Detroit he would insist "unless I wanted to have a regular Irish row that I should take up my old quarters" in his house.

John would set out on one of these expeditions with a list of purchases to be made and errands to be done, to which Charlotte's letters would add further commissions: "Please to get me a paper or box of black hairpins, such as ladies use. they can be had at any hairdressers. also the Comb, if you can remember the pattern which you left behind. If the St. Louis comes up in a day or two, . . . pray send *our shoes*. the boys are so hot in their thick soles, & I have not a pair to walk out in." Or at another time: "Now for a little list of several indispensible articles I forgot to speak about.

> 3 dozen pearl shirt buttons
> lots of shoe strings — a primer for Nony
> & as I had the misfortune to break one of the chimneys, I

send the size on the other side for you to get another, if you think proper. You left the clothes brush, although I had put it into your hat, had you not better get a new one?" Or again: "I have just been into the Cellar (*like a good little wife*) & find that we are on the last layer of our good butter, with but 5 lbs more in a crock . . . You had better therefore bring up some, also some few doz. Eggs if possible . . . we want a clothes line badly and 4 dozen clothes pins which you should get for *25 cents.*"

These mundane commissions reflect the petty household frictions of their daily living. Money matters sometimes created irritation between them. John controlled the purse, and Charlotte was always aware that he might disapprove of her expenditures. "I have *bought nothing*", she wrote him from Detroit; and then: "May I get a few pieces of Music at Morse's or McFarren's?" In their correspondence he was "good kind indulgent husband" and she was "dear little wife". Though she accepted unquestioningly a subordinate role, which was the usual marriage relationship in those days, still it sometimes left her irritable and fussy.

At the time when their fourth child was born they had been married nearly nine years. The early brightness of their happiness in each other was becoming shadowed now. John was making things no easier by sometimes finding fault with Charlotte and correcting her for her own good. Though he loved her fully, he was led by his perfectionism, the intensity of his convictions, to criticize her for too little zeal in the practice of a Christian life. Charlotte, the pious one! His harsh words lingered in her mind.

In the summer after Bertie's birth many things combined to make her particularly depressed: the certainty of never seeing England again, the long isolated winters in the frozen straits, the separation from friends in Monroe and Detroit. John was away on a trip to Detroit in June of that year, 1845, leaving her lonely and sorry for herself. Even the apartment next door in the Hill Quarters was empty at the time. When a returning officer, Lt. Spencer Norvell, arrived and moved in there, "it is some alleviation of my extreme loneliness to hear occasionally his step in the adjoining rooms." Norvell had come from the Sault, bringing her a letter from her friend Mrs. Merrill, who urged her in the strongest terms to come to the Sault for a visit. "She says 'I went to Captain Shook and he promised to give you a free passage. You must come. I have a room all prepared which is known by all here as Mrs. O'Brien's room. The boys have filled another with playthings for Lyster and Allan. If you do not come I shall be really offended, and will not write another word. Captain Merrill said last night, why does she not come, why should she stay there all alone. I shall go to the boat to meet you &c &c.' Of course I do not now go — unless you *permit*, and probably not then."

A few days later Charlotte wrote again: "By the last boat from the Sault I had another kind letter from Mrs. Merrill, again and again begging me to bring the children up, & saying that her boys count the days until they shall see their dear little playmates again, but I still wait for your return, or a letter of permission. Oh! that you had been generous enough to say to me 'you will be so lonely, dear Wife, of course you can go' — but I forebear . . . I shall again write a letter of postponement, tho' I really scarcely know what to say, as I am now ready, & she fully expects me.

"The weather is clear, but rather cold. I walk daily and try not to be lonely or unhappy, but do not always succeed. A very dark cloud has come over me, and I do not feel as I used to do — sometimes I sit & try to fathom what it is that has changed me so much. Then I endeavour to forget, but there are some words yet ringing in my ears that frighten me yet by their harsh and bitter sound, & then my heart grows hard again, & I seem to have no thought, no hope & no desire of anything in the world.

"But this is folly — the boat will be in, & I would not have you disappointed from silence at home. The dear dear boys are all well, & give me but little trouble. I trust that Providence will watch over & between us, perhaps better days will come. Believe me dear John to be always

Your dutiful & affec^{ate} Wife

C. O'Brien"

It was significant that she qualified her affection with that stiff word "dutiful". This was a period of ebb tide in their marriage. The heady excitement of love that had submerged their differences in their earlier years had subsided, exposing the shapes of their separate natures. John's doctrinaire idealism made him rigid and critical; Charlotte reacted with petulance and irritability. Her awareness of the clash of their characters had brought the dark cloud over her.

John was more patient than she, perhaps because he was so sure of the rightness of his own motives and conduct. He justified himself in his ponderous way: "You have at times called me selfish and unkind. They were epithets wrongly applied, the motive was misunderstood that called them forth. If I felt aggrieved that my

32

The Hill Quarters drawn in 1875 by Sergeant H. Heintz.

Charlotte fell short of that standard of christian prudence and meekness which none knew better how to attain — my error was more the result of love than of unkindness. I knew you possessed qualities of a sterling kind ...''

The fault in their quarrels may have been Charlotte's as much as his. She would feel neglected and sorry for herself and would reproach him unfairly: ''I was delighted to have your brief letter, but disappointed that you did not think to send me a pair of Shoes as I am really bare footed, neither did you ever leave me so *bare* of every thing as this time — not a potatoe in the house nor a bit of sugar, or rice, not a candle nor a piece of soap not *one* egg not a drop of ink, not a pen, or knife to cut one if I had it!!!! but by great luck I found this *one* sheet of paper. I however got Connif to get me what was also lately necessary, & have borrowed some ink which is *so* bad that I have to dip this miserable pen at every other word, & when I have done my letter, I have neither *sealing wax nor wafer*!!!!!''

Afterward she would repent of such an outburst, for self-criticism was instinctive in her; and she was soon writing again in a different tenor. ''Yesterday afternoon I walked through the sun & dust to the Post-office ... I was rewarded by Robert's handing me your last kind letter, written in the good old affectionate style ... Never let *fancies*, very false fancies whatever they may be, again induce you to think for one moment that you have not a devoted, & most affectionate little Wife, whose greatest sorrow is that she should ever vex or grieve so dear, so indulgent a husband.''

So the dark cloud gradually dispersed. Charlotte learned to accept the inevitable frictions of marriage with humor and love and could sum it all up by writing ''come home soon dear tiresome good kind husband to your most affectionate wife C. OB.''

The earliest photograph of Mackinac Island, July 1856. Judge Samuel Abbott's home is on the left and the O'Briens lived in Fort Mackinac just to the left of the flag pole.

The love between them was always strong beneath the surface disturbances. When they were apart they missed each other intensely; she would write "Never was there so dismal a place as this is rendered by your absence." Aside from John's absence, though, there really was little cause for loneliness. She had friends aplenty on the Island, who sought her out. One was Mrs. Henry Selby, who lived on "the farm" and sometimes came in her carriage to take Charlotte out for a ride to that open tract of cultivation in the midst of the forest. Mrs. Selby solicitously "makes me send for milk every morning." Mrs. Abbott was another who had taken a great liking for the Chaplain's pretty young English wife. She too would call in her carriage and invite Charlotte for long drives. She and Judge Abbott, having no children, took an interest in the O'Brien boys and made them welcome at their home, a stately white house with a two-story Doric portico and columned wings overlooking the shabby squalor of Market Street. Even though Mrs. Abbott was a Roman Catholic, she became Charlotte's best friend in the village. One day she took little Nony O'Brien, then not quite four, to a service at her church, "and such an account as he gave of the 'vespers' you never heard in your life," said Charlotte. Lyster explained more fully, "Nony went with Mrs. Abbott to her church on sunday afternoon, and he told us that the priest had a nightgown on."

Silas Casey — A graduate of West Point in 1826, Captain Casey was 38 when he took command of the garrison at Fort Mackinac in 1845. He remained there until he left to join Gen. Scott's army in Mexico.

In the garrison Charlotte's first close friend was Melinda Scott whose husband, Captain Martin Scott, was Commandant in the early years of the O'Briens' residence. This was a friendship that continued after the Scotts left Mackinac. Mrs. Scott would return to stay with the O'Briens, or Charlotte would visit her in Milwaukee.

After Martin Scott, Captain Silas Casey took charge as Commandant. Charlotte considered him an able officer: "he is quite determined, but very genial, winking at *little* deviations, but not for a moment giving way to contumacious offenders." This comment was prompted by Casey's dealing with a soldier named Harrison, who had made trouble about policing the O'Briens' quarters. The Captain "told him that if he heard anything more of his interference in any matter, he should march out of the garrison a great deal quicker then he ever walked into it."

Silas Casey and John O'Brien, being two Irish Episcopalians, were congenial friends. When in the summer of 1847, during the Mexican War, Casey and his company of the 2nd Infantry were withdrawn from Mackinac and sent to join the army advancing upon the City of Mexico, they exchanged letters. John exhorted the Captain to place his confidence in God; "he is the God of providence, as well as grace." Casey in his reply described the fighting

Lewis Cass

as the army approached the city, and told how in the battle of Churubusco "after remaining exposed to a heavy fire of Cannon and musketry, for more than an hour, [we] carried the works. I was the first man of the Reg in, followed by the Colours."

"War is a terrible evil," Captain Casey concluded, "and to the true follower of Christ, many things are constantly transpiring which are uncongenial to his feelings . . . That God may guide, guard and direct you through life, and sustain you in the trying hour of death is the prayer of your friend and Christian Brother S Casey."

Captain Casey's regulars had been replaced at Mackinac by a company of Michigan Volunteers, called the Brady Guards, commanded by Captain Morgan Gage. Charlotte had been apprehensive of their arrival. "I am afraid the 'Guards' will wear a *dark* if not a *black* uniform, quite a different set of men to what they used to be I am told, but it is useless to anticipate trouble." Actually the volunteers proved to be, with a few exceptions, an orderly and respectable company. After the Mexican War ended, they were withdrawn from Fort Mackinac and disbanded in June, 1848.

For a number of months the Fort remained abandoned, though the O'Briens were permitted to occupy their quarters till fall. This was a time of deep anxiety for them, for John was without a job. He went to Detroit to consult Charles Trowbridge, whose influence in Washington might secure him a Chaplain's appointment in the Navy. He thought of asking help from General Cass again, but decided that would be "out of place as well as out of taste" at this time when Cass was the Democratic candidate for the Presidency. "He reads no papers, opens no letters, and interferes not in any degree with politics — no pledges, no promises — and I think he is wise. If he be elected, then would be the time to make application."

This was a trying time for Charlotte, alone with her children in the vacant Fort. She wrote to John: "I have much ado to keep my mind easy and happy, I fear too much, & hope too little. May the gracious Lord who hath hitherto been so very gracious to us, direct us to a haven of peace. Yesterday, after sitting many hours at home, attending to the boys, and sewing, I took them all out on Fort Holmes, and while they picked strawberries which are now abundant, I sat under a tree, alternately reading and thinking of you. Every little while one would exclaim, 'How I wish Papa was here'. Never was a place so lonely, it is *Solitude* indeed — if I stay long thus, I think I shall fall into an eerie sort of life, and be half the time wandering in the woods with the children . . . I wish above all things to be where a door of great usefulness may be opened for you together with such a competency as may make you more easy. Let us commit all into His hands, whose Servant you are."

Mackinac at mid-century.

Though the garrison was gone, she still had many friends on the Island to relieve her loneliness. Two of them came up one day to invite her and her older boys to a Fourth of July picnic on Round Island. In a party of fifteen or more, "we started at 2 oclock in a large batteau . . . & we really had a pleasant trip. & such delicious cake, & ice cream, & charlotte ruse, & strawberries & coffee, & almmonds & raisins, & *wine* & *B*, & lemonade and such quantities of chicken & tongue, & sandwiches, & oceans of cream for all!! all that was wanted was *you*, yes *you* . . . at any rate, it raised for a while my sad spirits, and for the dear children it was all unmixed delight."

John's quest for new employment was fruitless, but after several months the anxious time ended. A company of the 4th Infantry, under command of Captain Charles H. Larnard, reoccupied the Fort in November, 1848, and the Rev. Mr. O'Brien's appointment was renewed.

For no one was this a more happy outcome than for the O'Brien boys. To them the Island was a very paradise in which to grow up. The patterned military routine of the Fort, the freedom of the wild woods behind, the gravelly beaches where little waves expired with a hushing sound, the medley of humanity in the village — fishermen, boatmen, Indians, woodsmen — it was a world complete of all a boy's desire. In the gardens below the Fort they had their own plots, where they grew vegetables. They kept chickens and ducks in pens behind their house. They sailed toy sailboats on the lake in summer and skated on it in winter. They watched the side-wheel steamboats that came "from below", "from above", and could name them all afar: the Western, the Keystone, the Baltic, the Wisconsin.

The Fort gardens as seen from the fort.

Sultana

Ralph K. Roberts

There was no school in the Fort, nor any in the village that their parents could approve of. John himself took charge of their education. They studied at home all morning and then recited their lessons to him or to their mother. They learned to write clearly and neatly and to read the Bible. They studied English history; Lyster said "I like King Alfred the best of any king that I have yet read of." There is a glimpse of their training in arithmetic in a letter John wrote them from Detroit: "I had a very pleasant passage down. The Niagara passed Fort Gratiot on Wednesday afternoon at 5 OC having run from Mackinac to that place in eighteen hours & 30 minutes; the distance is 250 miles. How many miles an hour did the Niagara run? Can you tell Allan if not Lyster can calculate and tell you."

By the time Lyster was ten he could write his father a presentable letter, in spite of distraction by his mother's talkative callers in the parlor where he was writing:

"My dear father

We are all well, but we are very lonely without you. We study our lessons in the morning, and after we have said them to mamma, we go out to play till the baby wakes, and then we take care of him by turns . . . Noel says that you must buy him a drum but Allan says that you must not spend your money in such foolish toys. The Empire has broken her rudder, in trying to get the Sultana off a reef of rocks on which she ran last night in the fog, and was a very long while coming into the dock. I will try to take care of all you put me in charge of, and I will to do all that you tell me when you return home. Old Qack and his wives are quite well, the yellow hen

Empire

Ralph K. Roberts

has brought eight chickens from sixteen eggs, one of which died . . .
I have now told you all that I can think of and remain

my dear papa
your dutiful son Lyster M. Obrien''

Two years later when the baby, Bertie, was big enough to run with the rest of them, ''On Thursday us four boys went down to Robert Carney's and we made a tent on the hill above his house, and we baked some potatoes, and we had fine sport. On Friday Mrs Carney gave a party and we went down too, and they acted some tableaux which were very entertaining. Bertie is a great pet at the major's he has slept there for the the last two nights . . . Mama wants you to get six pounds of macaroni and a bag of table salt dont forget to bring us our skates.''

Arch Rock from the water.

B. C. Morse, Jr.

"The major" was Captain Larnard, the new Commandant, who was a Major by brevet and liked to be addressed by that title. He was a widower, but he had a large family living with him: his mother, his two sisters and his two daughters. It was they who made a pet of little Bertie.

In the spring of that year, 1849, the Major had thrown the O'Briens' household into disruption by arranging to have the Hill Quarters repainted, both the O'Briens' apartment and the vacant one next door. At the same time the Larnards were refurnishing their own rooms in the stone building across the parade ground. Because their kitchen was out of order, the whole Larnard family took their meals with the O'Briens for several weeks, trooping up to the Hill Quarters three times a day. The Major loaned his own servant, James, to assist Charlotte and her maid, Ellen, with the cooking and serving, and assigned two soldiers to help with the heavier work. Even so, "setting three formal tables in a day" for the combined families was a tiresome labor. "I grew oh! so weary of that never ending cooking and providing", Charlotte said.

The painters working in and around the house added to the confusion. While their own rooms were being painted, the O'Briens all had to sleep in the adjoining quarters. The "odious smell of the paint" gave Charlotte headaches. When John embarked for a trip to Detroit, "I was in so much pain & distress from my head when you left & indeed the whole of that day that I scarcely knew what I was about, and very much fear you attributed my silence to coldness and indifference to your leaving me. after you started . . . I then lay down in my room for half an hour, and failing to obtain sleep, I rose to look after the boat — finding to my great surprise that she was but just leaving. I threw on my bonnet & shawl, & hastened to the ramparts, & there sat on the wall, & waved my handkerchief a long time, but as you did not show yours, I am afraid you did not see me, & this I regretted very much."

The next morning, happily, the Larnards' new cookstove and other matters arrived, and at noon they dined with the O'Briens for the last time. After dinner, as a token of thanks, the Major and his mother took Charlotte and her boys for a ride out on the lake as far as the Arched Rock in the government Mackinac boat with a number of rowers. By the end of the day the Larnards' quarters had been so comfortably settled that "a polite invitation arrived from them for me & Lyster to go to tea with them".

The O'Briens' house was still in "a perfect uproar" with the painting but, Charlotte wrote, "you may be sure with what joy I find myself once more *alone* with our dear boys, there possitively seems nothing to do about the house now . . . although I do not look or feel quite rightly yet because of the paint . . . I am disposed to think that a constant crowding of the every day cares of life are neither beneficial to my temper nor general character. I love perhaps too well, to be quiet & retired, to have time for thought at home, & for walking abroad.''

Quiet did not return. The very next day the ''insolent conduct'' of her servant, Ellen, determined Charlotte to put up no longer with her ''sullen and violent temper. I think that she has lived with me quite long enough, & I do not feel at all inclined to keep her . . . Never was there so insolent and at the same time so inefficient a woman.'' Whether or not Ellen's temper was an excusable result of those trying weeks of the Larnards, Charlotte asked John to bring back another girl from Detroit. She thought he might accomplish this more easily than usual, because of the hot midsummer weather in the city.

Under these domestic stresses Charlotte's headaches continued, and she had a cold aggravated by the paint. ''I am still extremely unwell, my chest very very sore, and my throat too, especially the roof of my mouth.'' Her health had indeed never been robust. Even in the happy time of her honeymoon, years before, she had suffered from headache and ''indisposition'' that sometimes kept her in bed all day. She seems always to have been frail and subject to illnesses. Now, on top of it all, she was having trouble with her teeth. She decided to go to Detroit to consult a dentist. After John returned, bringing a new servant, Elizabeth, she went down and stayed with Bishop and Mrs. McCoskry. It was planned that she would later bring the McCoskry's daughter, Mary, back to Mackinac with her for a visit.

Bishop Samuel A. McCoskry

42

Having left John and the boys in a house still in much confusion, Charlotte could not clear housekeeping concerns from her mind. She wrote John a letter of instructions: "Please to tell Elizabeth to take up the crumb cloth now & then to shake — but on no account let it *remain up* — & pray take care of the parlour matting — & the carpet in our room also — nail those little pieces down, if you have not done so, & let the celler be attended to, & that good butter put away in some safe corner — get a mouse trap just into the dark closet upstairs — and be sure to have the flour & meal covered — I found two mice in the barrel the day after Ellen left — she left all exposed — get that bedstead nicely fixed, made up with common sheets for the children a day or two previous to my return, there will be nothing to go on it but the straw bed now on, over which must be put a thick comforter. I shall send the mattress up, and a bag of feathers for two pillows which Elizabeth can *make & fill* . . . please to have one small trout pickled — it is to be simply boiled first as if for dinner — & then scalding vinegar poured over with spices — cloves & allspice — you had better have one for dinner someday, & experiment on what happens to be left — *pray* my dear keep dear Bertie's *sun*-bonnet on, & Nony's hat — I shall get them all a staw hat . . . when the mattress comes you will put it on our bed, with the straw bed underneath, & put the feather bed *under* & the old mattress at top in the other little room where Mary is to sleep — I am sure my dear husband will attend to these matters, as it will save so much confusion and me so much trouble — this I know is not a *nice* letter, but I had so much of business matters to fill it up . . ."

There was more, and John might well have replied as he did on a later occasion of the sort, "Your list of directions embracing different matters which if you were at home would not & could not be accomplished in six months, how do you think that I could do them in two weeks."

Before he had time for any such reaction, a second letter arrived from Charlotte. The situation was entirely changed. Bishop McCoskry had been ill, and his doctors insisted on his going to Mackinac for a month; "so *we all come* next week . . . they bring their cook, & I shall get another girl if I possibly can. We must give the B. & Mrs. *our room*, & Mary the other, & go ourselves upstairs with *all the children* — if you possibly can, have the wardrobe *taken up*, also the couch, I shall bring a cheap new washstand . . . we shall have a *hard* summer my dear, but if I see you happy, I shall not mind anything — pray let it all be as neat as you can, especially the children, & if you cannot manage that keep them out of sight till I rig them up — if you have only a fish in the house we shall do grandly — Farnsworth *pulls 5 of my teeth out* on Saturday so I shall return *without any* and be without till sep.br — will you or can you love me while I look so ugly? he found it impossible to do anything with them & they all advise this course."

So lately freed from "never ending cooking and providing" while boarding the Larnards, and ailing so often that she "was confined to my bed more than half of the ten days I was in the city", she could not see this new visit as a happy prospect. For John it was otherwise. He was ecstatic.

"Tell the Bishop I have not heard of an event for the last seven years, which has been to me a source of more real heart felt joy than the tidings you last letter conveyed, that he & Mrs. McC. (whose praise is in all the churches) and their accomplished daughter were to grace by their presence and enliven by their fascinating powers the humble dwelling of the Chaplain at Mackinac. To carry, beloved, your suggestions into effect, I went instantly and vigorously to work, yes most cheerfully for it was a work of love, and that renders all labour light. It was an easy and agreeable task — for two reasons. It was executing the wishes of the sweetest and most amiable of wives, whom in spite of her teeth I must value esteem and love. Then there was no common pleasure in the thought that the preparations I was making in my domicile were to render it as fit abode as circumstances would allow, for guests of high degree."

At the joyous prospect, John dropped all thought of economy. Grandly he flung away the leash with which he had usually curbed Charlotte in her expenditures. "I fear your money will be run out," he told her. "You can call Mr. Hicks who will give you *whatever* you require. should he be absent ask friend Trowbridge or Baldwin and should either of them advance the sum you want I will have it transmitted with many thanks on your return. Dearest little wife, get what you want from any of the above, it will afford your loving husband pleasure to repay, whatever contributes to the happiness of his sweet Charlotte."

For once all the world was beautiful for John. Especially Mackinac Island. A bubbling exuberance enlivened his elaborate literary style.

"The weather now is delightfully charming. Thermometer now stands at 70° tho' it is 2 OC. The breeze, to say it is refreshing does not convey the balmy bracing invigorating influence diffusing itself thro every nerve and sinew, vein and muscle, bones flesh and marrow that form the constituent elements of the outward and material man. Description falls short of the reality, how much more must any effort of my sluggish genius and long dormant muse. You must be here to breathe and inhale this pure atmosphere yourself — the vigour it will impart, the unconscious bounding it gives the frame — between ourselves you may tell the Bishop, it will put his episcopal gravity to the test to keep his feet in a slow measured and dignified movement. The truth is I find a kind of skipping motion a most unaccountable propensity to beat time to tunes well known by a Reighley or a Kelly, called Patricks day & Tally hiho the grinder."

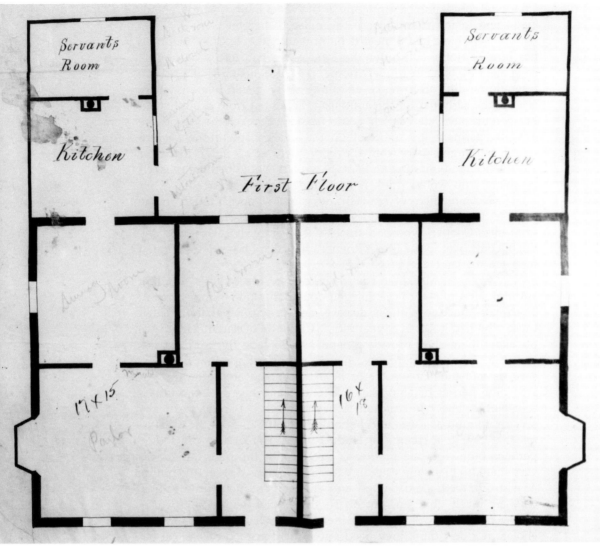

Floor plan of the Hill Quarters drawn in 1875

If the McCoskrys' visit was pure pleasure for John, it must have been no little strain on Charlotte, with the two families crowded together for a month. Again she had to set "three formal tables in a day". Fortunately the adjoining quarters were still vacant, providing room where the servants could stay, Elizabeth and the McCoskrys' cook.

In that summer of 1849 Mackinac Island was more thronged with visitors than usual, for there was an epidemic of cholera throughout the country and people escaping from the cities came to the cool northern climate. However poor her own health was,

Charlotte could not be unhappy if she had many friends about; loved and loving friends were the pulse of her life.

"We have had a most delightful summer . . ." she wrote to her brother, John Tull, after the McCoskrys had left. "We are all so spoiled by our most lovely home, & salubrious air that I believe it would be difficult to make us think that we could live anywhere else. in the early part of the summer we suffered from drought, but heavy rains have lately fallen, & our Island is again clothed in beauty as with a garment, it is undoubtedly the loveliest spot in the western world, although, apart from the Fort, there is no inducement for a residence, and our long and severe winters would be little relished by many who would think it in summer a perfect Arcadia."

No hint there of homesickness for England! though in the same letter to her brother she mentioned that she still heard often from Eliza Cooper, who had suggested recently that some day she might come over to see the O'Briens; "how can I be grateful enough for such a friend as she has been to me."

Even on Mackinac Island there were cases of cholera that autumn, all confined to the village population, none in the garrison. There was much fear of the disease, and people generally avoided those who had it. "It is a great pity", Charlotte declared, "that people allow themselves to feel so panic struck, as to fly from the sick bed of a neighbour, surely we have a stronger hope that God will save us and ours, if we try to help those who are suffering."

She herself had no fear. "I accidentally heard of the illness of a mother and two children, & went to see if I could be of any service. I found as I was told I should, the little ones in the greatest need of care & a change of clothes, one I think must die today, perhaps both — & the mother is very sick — the poor father was very thankful to me for attending to his little ones. I staid two hours, & with Elizabeth's aid bathed and changed the poor little things. they are lovely children, but oh so shamefully neglected, so dirty too, & no doctor will go to see them — they have no symptom of cholera nor do I think they need any thing but good care & proper food, but I fear my little efforts are too late to save their lives."

Whether or not a doctor would go to see the sick made little enough difference in those days, as the Larnards learned when the Major's mother became ill with an "attack of acute quinsy" in the spring of 1850. The Major said he had not seen her so ill for the last twenty years; but Dr. Joseph B. Brown, the Post physician, who attended her on April 29th, said that her illness though severe was by no means serious; she would be up in a few days. On the night of the 30th she died. The state of medical knowledge was pathetically low at the midpoint of the century.

Dr. Joseph Bullock Brown photographed in 1858

At the time when Mrs. Larnard died, Charlotte, accompanied by Lyster, was away visiting Mrs. Scott in Milwaukee. She heard from John about the "melancholy event", how the Major and his daughters, weeping, had spent part of the day with him on the hill, and how he, Mrs. Abbott and Mrs. Selby had "made every necessary arrangement and discharged the last mournful office."

In the same letter John also reported a happier item of news: that their servant Eliza, who had spent the winter with them, had agreed to remain for the summer as well. This was good news indeed, for there had always been too much change of servants. Teen-age girls mostly, they would work for a few months, Charlotte would train them in cooking and housework, and then they would restlessly depart. So Elizabeth, who had replaced the insolent Ellen, had stayed through the pleasant months of summer and autumn but had gone home before winter set in. It was hard to get any help in the winter.

But then Eliza had come back; she had worked for Charlotte before; and they were fond of one another. She lived with the O'Briens through the winter and looked forward to spending the summer with them too. But first she wanted to visit her mother briefly, so after Charlotte's return from Milwaukee, Eliza went down to Detroit in late May.

John was in the city at that time also, staying with Bishop McCoskry and buying crockery, clothing and provisions. He was arranging for Eliza's passage back to Mackinac when unexpectedly her mother refused to let her go; "her sister was to be married, and her mother would not on any account consent to be left alone." Knowing how disappointed Charlotte would be, John did his best to recruit a replacement. He spent two days "in looking up a gal". "I have been in as many houses in the suburbs of the city as if I was appointed by the U. States to take the census. I felt rather awkward on Saturday evening standing nearly opposite Cass's speaking with two girls. I suppose my character will sustain me. After this tour of reconnoitering the outskirts of the city, I think my knowledge of it exceeds the bishops."

Interior of Fort Mackinac about 1871. The Hill Quarters is at the top center.

At last with Eliza's help he found a girl, Ann, who was willing to go — one of the many refugees from the potato famine in Ireland. "I understand she is a good natured girl." He agreed to pay her 12 shillings a week — three dollars — and sent her off to Mackinac with his letter. What happened next appears in Charlotte's reply. She met the boat.

"I have just succeeded in digesting the annoyance caused by the arrival of a stranger, instead of Eliza — I was at first inexpressibly disappointed especially as a host of vexations seemed to have accompanied the advent of our new 'help'. Heaven save the mark, for the first thing she did was go to bed & groan, & there she now lies, a second but more bulky edition of the green Mary of 1849, but her illness gives me no very deep concern — she has been seasick, but has all the appearance of health, & I rather like her face — it is Irish and honest in expression, & that she is not especially blessed with beauty is no great fault, but the silly thing has let her largest trunk go on with the boat to Chicago, & tells me she has two straw hats of mine in it — this is really vexatious."

Next day: "Ann has had a terrible ague fit. Dr. B. has just administered an emetic, & the poor thing appears very tractable and quiet, but *I* am as you may suppose almost tired to death." Charlotte reluctantly sent Ann back to Detroit, carrying a letter to John. "she told me she had *fits once*, & felt as if she was going to have them again — had it not been for this, I think I would not have let her go."

With no servant the next week was toilsome for Charlotte, even though the Major sent a soldier, Haterick, to help her, and Mrs. McGuire, a soldier's wife who was living in the blockhouse nearby on the hill, was only too glad to get her washing and ironing. Then, unexpectedly, "This morning a girl made her appearance in the shape of a thickset ignorant *native*, ('to the very manner born') of your dear country. She came here to her brother Michail Morrison, who paid her passage from home, has only been in the country 5 months, and is greener than the greenest shamrock of dear old Ireland. however, I installed her forthwith at the rate she demanded $6 per month . . . we may as well try this specimen as it will save the passage of another, and yet, if an intelligent Protestant girl should come in your way, I should not hesitate to hire her in preference. this girl is cousin to the O'Malleys, & Darkins, I could never expect to keep her out of that set, and how long will they suffer her to remain with me? probably just long enough for me to take all the trouble of teaching her, and then they will coax her away or marry her to some twentieth cousin. She does not look healthy although large, and really seems about half witted, tho very ready and well able to clean and scrub about."

A visitor more welcome than the Irish servant girls came to the Island at this time. He was a piano tuner, who tuned both Charlotte's piano and the Larnards'. Hers, the tuner said, sounded more brilliantly than the Major's, and she herself thought it was "wonderfully improved, it is soft & mellow, & it is a delight to play on it."

All her world was lovely in these days of early summer, "every thing around us so still and serene, the weather most unspeakably beautiful. Last evening I went from one window to another, & thought the view from each was more exquisite than I had ever thought it before." The Island was "now clad in all the leafy adornments of the month of June — one rain converted it as by the touch of a magician's wand into the most fragrant and shady paradise."

In the interim between the Irish girls, while she was without a servant, the Larnards "had the grace to insist on my taking all my meals there, & invited Lyster also. I have been therefore to dine with Annie several times while her brother was gone (he returned this morning). yesterday we took our supper in the woods, it being a very lovely day, so warm and bright. we got the waggon and went to the woods by the red barn, and while Katy & James *set the table*, we went down to Col. Scott's old pic-nic ground — you remember the little dear meadowlike opening, the tent stakes alone were there to trace out the spot he chose with so much good taste, but I soon left it, for to me it was all haunted ground, round which the friends of bygone days were flitting — poor Sophy Biddle, & Byrne, & Scott, & sweet Jane Stuart — the living & the dead, with a crowd of others."

The next day Major Larnard and his sister Annie came up to spend the evening with her. They wanted to sing, but Annie could not manage the accompaniments. So Charlotte sat down at the newly tuned piano and played, and they sang, and afterward "the Major condescended to say that I kept such admirable time, that he wished we would practice in that way, as it would improve her — *wonderful concession*, when she has had *no* teaching and my music cost more than the whole of her education." Charlotte was always the proud English lady, well aware of her breeding and culture. Her letter to John continued, "My piano is as sweet as a silver bell — so clear yet soft, and so it ought indeed to be for the expense was enormous $17.75. I fear you will be horrified, but I will try with all my heart to economize in other ways."

In John's absence her oldest boy, Lyster, now thirteen, was increasingly a help and pleasure to her. He "has been very very useful & good", though the younger ones, Nony and Bertie, were "two regular little rovers and rowdies as ever were made". When she had a headache one evening, "Lyster made me a cup of tea all himself as late as ten, and rubbed my head a long time with camphire . . . it must have been past 11 when the dear boy left me to go to bed." He had become a serious and responsible young man, an example to his little brothers, as his mother had always instructed him to be — "they will do what they see you do, & they will say what they hear you say."

The Hill Quarters from the southwest

Allan was in Detroit with their father at this time, and Lyster wrote him a letter. "I was very lonely the first day you were away but I have got accustomed to it and I do not feel so now. I suppose you were disappointed in not hearing from me before. I began to copy a letter the day before yesterday to you but as I happened to look out of the window I saw the Louisiana coming. Mama had just time to finish her letter and I to take it down before the mail was closed. The seeds in our garden have come up and are growing very fast . . . Two of the men have deserted. Flint and Katsby, they went up on a propellor on Saturday night. My ball is not much use to me now, and my knife takes its place and sees good service. The other day I made a waggon for the boys, and for a time it was splendid, but by and by Bertie brought it to me with one of the wheels gone and the railing broken, it is quite discouraging to me to have the things I make broken in this fashion. I intend to make some jackstraws and several other things, which you will see when you come home . . . We had a fine time unpacking the barrels and then trouble for the dishes had to be washed and wiped and put away, the girl sick in bed and groaning as Mama says like a steam engine."

The barrels were some that John had sent from Detroit with the Irish girl, Ann, one with crockery, another with nine hams, and a box with clothing for the boys — "costly robes for the scions of a not degenerate house may they be better and wealthier than their parent."

"Well, my love," Charlotte wrote him, "we have been very busy, unpacked & washed every article of crockery, nothing broken, & I am now writing by the relighted lamp, whose new chimney gives us once more a most brilliant light. I am very much pleased with all you have sent . . . I have many many times . . . wished you were at my side to hear how pleased I was . . . it is now raining gloriously, & the air is perfumed as with the breath of a thousand flowers. your garden seeds are much choked with weeds, had you not better bring a hoe, so that we need not be always borrowing? . . . If you *can* get me a pretty pair of round toed slippers as well as the gaiters please to do so . . . God ever bless you best & dearest of husbands ever prays your affec^ate Charlotte"

She had passed through restiveness into contentment in her marriage with John. When their differing personalities caused friction between them, Charlotte was the one who yielded, bending her ways to his and curbing her irritability. She was determined to be "your dear little wife . . . bad as she is, & well as she feels she is not half good enough for you." Oh, she would flare up occasionally, but never for long. "I was so naughty the day I left home, but you must forget my petulence for the nine hundred & ninety ninth time, and I will be so sweet and good when I come home that you will find your reward."

John, ever sure of his rectitude, made no such concessions. He was always patient with her — that attitude itself could be annoying — but he never suggested that he was wrong about anything. He testified his love for her in his own oratorical way: "Love . . . more than I can express for her whose happiness temporal & spiritual absorbs every thought and faculty of my soul." "What shall I say to you — no terms can convey my feelings, my love my affections — all are yours." Though verbose this was utterly sincere, and she knew that.

John's appearance in middle age was of dignity and solemnity, even of sadness. "You tell me not to look gloomy or sad. I pledge my word not to be so — but remember my moods and feelings take their complexion from the world in which I live — and who is to disperse from my horizon, the sombre tints & the dark clouds that lour at times around and above it; Who can do it, but one who is the joy, the light and solace of that little world I call my home. Then dearest let us look to the future with hope and let the past be consigned to the land of forgetfulness — let our contest be for the time to come — a contest of love."

He wore glasses nowadays, small rimless lenses that had a tendency to tip sidewise out of level, and he wore a wig of dark brown slightly touseled hair. The aspect he had had in his twenties, of an eager, confident, young missionary, had changed in his forties to the look of a stern but kindly schoolmaster. Disappointment and frustration in his profession had discouraged him. He seldom went

Let Eldus 'sweet little wife accept the undivided attachment of her devoted husband — JOB

John O'Brien — From a daguerreotype made about 1848, when he was in his early 40's.

any more to the diocesan conventions that he used to attend so assiduously, cultivating friendships that might lead to advancement.

Charlotte would try to encourage him: "Everyone thinks so highly of your preaching & speaks so well of you, that I think you are totally wrong in the supposition that you could not get a parish." On an occasion when Bishop McCoskry took him to a convention at Pontiac, she was glad. "I knew the Bishop would insist upon it, & I know you will preach better, & that you will be the best & boldest & handsomest too of all the long black-robed gentlemen assembled there — the least in debt either, & the least evil spoken of, so hold up your head dearest. tho many many have a better wife than you *have* had, *no one* has so good a husband as I, unworthy as I feel myself to be of such a blessing."

There was always a lurking anxiety in the back of her mind that John's Chaplaincy might not be continued, particularly upon a change of Commandants. Once, shortly after the Fort had been reoccupied in 1848 and Major Larnard had reappointed him, the Secretary of War had ordered Mackinac stricken from the list of posts to which Chaplains were allowed. At that sudden crisis Charlotte had written in great distress to Mrs. Cass. The few inhabitants of the Island, she said, were unable to support a Protestant minister; "they as well as the Garrison, will be hereby utterly deprived of all the religious privileges they have hitherto enjoyed. I would not say much of my dear husbend, whom you may perhaps kindly remember, knowing that you will better imagine than I can describe his regret in the prospect of leaving a spot, which whatever may be its disadvantages as a place of residence, he prizes so much as a field in which he can labour amongst the citizens as a Missionary indeed, without money and without price, literally seeking not *theirs* but *them*. Indeed *all* seem to share in the sorrow which this unexpected order has occasioned, and *some* have whispered that *one word* from *Gen. Cass* on this subject to Sec^{ty} Marcy (who has the nomination of the Posts, and who, perhaps, is not fully aware of the claims of this one to a Chaplain) will restore it to the enjoyment of those benefits resulting from the previous arrangement."

Whether the General indeed spoke to the Secretary is not recorded, but Fort Mackinac was restored to the list.

In her unobtrusive way Charlotte had made a notable place for herself at Mackinac. To her pleasant airy house on the high ground of the Fort everybody, friends or strangers, made a call. Visiting officers and summer vacationers paid their respects. "Mrs. Kearney & Medora called on me yesterday, also Gen. Churchill, who inspected the troops." "I had a call from a very fine looking man, of elegant manners, the Very Revnd Mr. Kilsaley." "Capt. Gore & Mr. Jones did themselves the honour to call upon me." They came to see Mr. O'Brien too, of course, but teas and social talk were not his forte. His beautiful, gentle wife with her sensitive response to people, her cultivated English speech and manners, was the stronger

TOWN OF MACKINAC, ON LAKE HURON, STATE OF MICHIGAN.

Mackinac Island harbor in 1856

attraction. In an informal way she was the lady of Fort Mackinac. While Commandants' wives came and went, Mrs. O'Brien remained, loved and admired. If you did not see her, you had missed something at Mackinac.

This is not to say that she was over-cordial. She maintained a proper British reserve toward people who were too forward. When the Rev. Mr. Joseph Large called — "what a pompous person he is! I was very dignified and polite, he trying to pass for an old friend while I quietly reminded him I had *once* had the pleasure of seeing him! . . . [He] obligingly told me he was agreeably disappointed in Mackinac as he had expected to find it nothing but a *barren rock*!!"

The Bramble Wreath — September 12, 1840, when this drawing was made, was Charlotte's 28th birthday.

Charlotte had had no control over the fate that plucked her out of a comfortable life in England and cast her onto the American frontier, to live there in straitened circumstances. What she could and did control was her own behavior, leading her life with courage, good humor, generosity and kindness through easy times and hard. She was a lady of character and good breeding. People perceived her as such; thereby she made her mark in the world. Through those who knew her, most of all through her sons and her husband, she exerted the force of her spirit.

Her husband greatly needed her strengthening affection. He was prone to gloom and discouragement. I hope, my dear, she would write to him, "that I shall see you bright & cheerful, & *occasionally* at least, taking a glance at life through the rose coloured medium . . . we have certainly many many blessings, & I think we should try to make ourselves contented although clouds & dark skies do really at times darken our path: who ever expected it to be all sunshine above & flowers around was a fool, & not a man of sense. You know *we* are not so weak therefore let us hope for the best both of God, & of *each other* and of our dear boys also."

Though solemnity was John's usual mood, he could sometimes be aroused from it. He had a quite boyish interest in curiosities and shows. Once he wrote from Detroit to his sons, "I went on Saturday evening to the Diarama and saw many splendid views." These were illuminated pictures of such scenes as the Cathedral at Milan, Jerusalem and Mount Calvary, and Belshazzar's feast, "the most splendid and grandest view of all." Furthermore, he said, "There is in Detroit a Crockadile; it is said to be a very great curiosity. Such an animal is very seldom seen; and if I can spare a few shillings I will give them to see it."

Two days later, in a letter to Charlotte: ''Last Monday I spent a most charming evening at Trowbridge's and had the pleasure of an introduction with the celebrated Lover author of Handy Andy &c he sung several of his favorite songs with a character and expression no language of mine can describe. I forgot everything, was altogether in a whirl of laughter and fun, even the stately grandeur of Mrs Trowbridge was scattered to the winds of heaven . . . some of his comic, I mean Irish songs & recitations are so full of wit & humor . . . it is a hurricane of fun — it is a bedlam of hilarity, in which soul & mind and the material part of our existence are . . . confused and hurled together.''

Under John's outward clerical dignity there was a somewhat heavy-handed sense of humor. In the summer of 1851, when he took a steamboat trip to Buffalo, he was asked to chaperone the two Trowbridge girls, Eliza and Kate, who were also going there.

''We embarked accompanied by the band of the 4th Inf. whether in honour of the distinguished party alluded to, or that the band and the military staff of Detroit were under marching orders is of little consequence . . . Just as our carriage came in sight of the boat followed by two others, and as our prancing steeds with arched necks and foaming bits were reined up at the Ocean's gangway . . . the band on the hurricane deck instantly struck up a lively spirit-stirring air; had the incident occurred at another time or in a more sequestered place, I verily believe my feet would be found in motion lightly tripping on the fantastic toe those graceful evolutions acquired in happier days on Erin's verdant soil . . . As

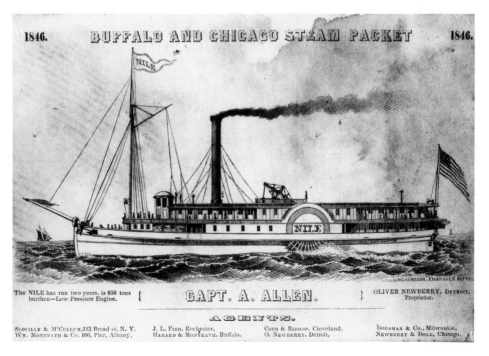

your humble servant entered the boat accompanied by a sweet look-ing and intellectual young lady leaning on his arm . . . the admiring crowd . . . cheered us onward with deafening shouts and waving hats on high. Whether these unsought honours were intended for me and my distinguished charge, or conferred on others less deserv-ing, I leave it to my kind indulgent friends to determine." Mani-festly, he loved it.

Having delivered his ladies to Buffalo, he crossed to Canada to visit a friend who was Rector of Niagara. "You have frequently heard me speak of the Revd Mr Creen, it was thro him I became acquainted with Sir John Coburn (now Lord Leaton)." At Mr. Creen's he met a young clergyman who was Rector of Waterloo and who invited him to come to that city to conduct services on Sunday. He did so, and then learned that his young host was to be married on Tuesday. Of course John stayed for the wedding. So he entered a rare and exhilarating experience, for he found himself a welcome guest at a fashionable affair. There he met a man whom he had wished for years to know, the Rev. Mr. Grasscet, Rector of Toronto, one of the most popular preachers in Canada; "he met me with all the cordiality of an old acquaintance, reaching out his hand he said, I have often heard of you through our mutual friends, and am glad of the present interview."

Mr. Grasscet officiated at the wedding ceremony, after which "All the invited guests proceeded to the residence of the bride's mother, where was one of the most elegantly furnished tables I have sat down to since I came to America." At the end of dinner, toasts were proposed, one following another in quick succes-sion, until presently came "the clergy of the Episcopal Church of the United States . . . I was in for it — a speech was to be made — as a preparatory step, I was on my legs — when hear hear resounded thro' the bannered hall & along the festive board. I could not resort to the hacknied exordium of being unacquainted with public speaking so . . . rushed in medias res of my subject, held the attention of my auditory for 6 or 7 minutes and concluded with a little oratorical flourish", toasting the faithful and eloquent Rector of Toronto. John may have been a little carried away by the cordiality and the wine, but his lengthy speech was applauded. He returned home glowing with the memory of having shared in a most distinguished occasion and "moved among the first circles".

Life at Mackinac was much more simple. While Charlotte took a trip to Milwaukee with Bertie in September, John stayed at home with the three older boys. His bachelor housekeeping was not elaborate. "We have got along as well as might be expected, living cheaply and very economically. Our breakfasts coffee & bread and butter — dinners very simple and teas if possible more so . . . I suppose you are so taken up with calling teaing and caking drinking perhaps beer that you care little how boys and I are getting on. Is it out of sight out of mind — if so, a different state exists here."

Fort Mackinac from the harbor. The fort garden is in the foreground.

But life at the Fort was not always dull. "On Wednesday night a number of men went into the garden and tore up about 300 heads of cabbage and a large quantity of the tomatoes, vegetable oysters, onions, cucumber vines && . . . The delinquents have been discovered and some are in the black hole and guardhouse. Black, Deets Brittain in black hole, Moran in guardhouse all for the garden affair; several for being drunk . . . I forgot to mention that they tore up by the roots several of the currant trees. I understand there are several others implicated in the garden concern but whether they will be punished for it or not I cannot say."

Just three days later John was sitting at his desk in the study when Nony, whom he had sent to get some potatoes from the garden, came into the house crying. Corporal Moran had stopped him at the sally port and refused to let him pass through. "I went down with the child at once to Major L[arnard] told the incident. He sent for Moran and in my presence he gave him a tremendous tonguing in his best style I mean language adapted to the impudent act Moran had committed." As Lyster expressed it, the Major "gave him a holing up for it, since then we have had no more trouble about going."

The Major got good marks for this incident, but an occurence the next day put him in less favor with the Rev. Mr. O'Brien. It was Sunday, and "to the scandal of some & the annoyance of others, a buggy was driven into the garrison by Scott during our service and while the last hymn was singing. Brevet Major Larnard and his wife sitting up in said buggy like one lashed to a perpendicular post drove bye." The Major had been remarried just a few months before to a Miss Eldridge of New York, and John was inclined to take a critical view of the family because Mrs. Eldridge, the bride's mother, who was visiting, had not been to church. "I can scarcely imagine that the woman is a professor, if she be, she must be a weak sister in Israel."

On Sunday a week later, though, when Mrs. Eldridge attended church twice, he decided that "she is a quiet good natured person, and if in another position would appear to more advantage." His morning discourse that Sunday had been "Ye shall reverence my Sabbaths". "In the evening the subject — slander — a spic & span new concern, coming down with a scorpion's tail on all slanderers tale bearers & willing listners. Some of the descriptions were true to life, they were applied no doubt by several to those of whose conduct they were striking portraitures ... It did hit hard, but unfortunately the chief delinquents were not hearers."

Tolerance was not among John's virtues. With the confidence of one who knows the desires and purposes of God, he condemned those modernists whose religious opinions differed from his own. "I am sick of hearing of the progress of the age . . . and that contemptible verbal cant assumed by a class of empty sciolists whose chief excellence consists in presumption and dogmatism . . . I hate the cant of that self-styled philosophic school, that overweening self complacency, that assumed height of intellect and metaphysical investigation it claims for itself."

So much for the "mis-called rational religion" of humanists, transcendentalists and such. He felt equal scorn for the opposite religious current of his time, the Oxford Movement, "Puseyism", which was reintroducing liturgy and rituals of ancient Catholicism into Church of England services. John himself was strictly a Bible Christian, Low Church, evangelical. He believed that man, made in the express image of God, shared not only his Creator's appearance but his immortality. "There is in the hearts of men a testimony that they shall live forever"; they "shrink back with horror at the thought of annihilation." Just when the life after death would begin was unclear. When Mrs. Larnard died, she had passed "into the presence of her God & Saviour." But at other times John envisaged that the dead would rise only when God "opens the heavens and calls you out of your graves to stand at his judgment seat."

After the judgment "his work of mercy is forever ended", for in the immortal life there would be no middle course. It would be spent in bland unremitting bliss around the throne of God or

The Mission Church where John frequently preached. By the 1840's the other buildings were the Mission House Hotel.

in medieval torment, "the horrors of that place where the worm dieth not & the fire is not quenched." To receive the better fate good conduct was not enough. Man was born a sinner, guilty and corrupt, and would inevitably fail to meet God's standards of impossible perfection. Salvation could be attained only through Christ, whose mercy must be begged in abject, humiliating abasement. John approvingly quoted Job, "I abhor myself", and Ezra, "I am ashamed and blush to lift up my face." He would not accept a man of dignity, self-respect, righteousness. Such a one was a Pharisee, "and the displeasure of God follows him." Man could not stand up in his integrity; he must crawl and grovel for mercy.

Such was the evangelical creed that John preached relentlessly all his life. As he grew older, though, his sermons became less harsh and dramatic. He threatened his congregations less, reasoned and pleaded with them more.

"You have heard of a Saviour, you have listened to his gospel which proclaims a free salvation, but perhaps you think you need it not. Take care lest this satisfaction with yourself may not be your ruin. May you be led by divine grace to give it up. May God enable every one now in his presence to utter this humble but blessed prayer — God be merciful to me a sinner!!!! Amen."

He kept his sermons neatly written in little pamphlets, carrying some of them with him when he travelled, so that he was always ready when invited to preach. Such an occasion arose in June, 1852, when he was visiting Washington, D.C. In that city he was asked to officiate in Sunday services at St. John's Church, and this he was pleased to do.

The reasons for his visit to the capital were several: to collect some back pay that was owed him, to try to get Lyster an appointment to West Point, and for himself to apply for a position as a Naval Chaplain. He called upon important people for their help. He had a letter of introduction from C. C. Trowbridge to his brother-in-law, the Honorable Henry Sibley. Sibley was one of the finest looking and most handsome men in the city, "the perfection of a man." He "received me with as much cordiality & warmth of friendship as if we were the most devoted and attached friends, took up the case of Lyster and said he would instantly go to work."

John was received with similar cordiality by his old friend Dr. S. Pyne, Rector of Christ's Church, who offered to see several of his Navy friends about the Chaplaincy. Dr. Pyne was "a man of great wealth and moves in the highest circles and intimate with many of the first & leading characters here." He invited John to dine " in a family way" with him and other gentlemen. "The dinner was elegant . . . there was a profusion of wines (French names) I neither understood nor could pronounce, tho' they were in abundance they were scarcely touched. It was after 6 OC when we left the table having gone to it after 5 OC. I met on this occasion with a gentleman an exceedingly accomplished man Secretary to the Brazilian committee of claims who has travelled a great deal visited the Island of Mackinac some years ago with which he was much delighted."

This was heady experience, being made welcome in great houses, meeting prominent and cultivated men. John was in his element. "If time allowed I could play the gentleman here for several months, & move in the very top circles."

After Dr. Pyne's dinner he went with his friend Captain John A. Whitall to spend the evening with the Captain's father, who "lives in a very elegant mansion & in good style." Mr. Whitall had been left a large fortune by the death of a southern relative — "fortunes may fall into the lap of men," John commented sadly to Charlotte, "& mitres be rained down from the skies but none will alight upon the pate of your John." Indeed this had been the pattern of his life, ever since those boyhood days with James Wright at Foulksrath Castle in Kilkenny: to be a friend of the rich and the great, but never to have what they had. And yet he knew his real happiness: "what does he want of fortune & of mitre when he already possesses the dearest & sweetest treasure his own lovd & loving Charlotte."

Mackinac Island harbor drawn in 1854 by Alfred R. Waud.

Except for the hospitality of the great, John got little for his efforts on this visit to Washington. Neither the Naval Chaplaincy nor Lyster's appointment to the Military Academy was ever realized.

If Lyster was disappointed, he was too busy to be much depressed. A more immediate excitement occupied his mind: his uncle John Tull was coming to visit Mackinac. Now that Lyster was fifteen he had taken up the manly sport of shooting pigeons, and he knew that Uncle John was a hunter too. He wrote urgently: "My dear Uncle, We were all happy to learn that you are coming here, and will you please bring up your gun with you, for we expect plenty of pigeons this summer, and I think we can tramp all over the Island with you after them? Come as soon as you can, we will be looking for you on every boat. Your affectionate nephew, Lyster O'Brien."

Charlotte was as excited as Lyster with plans for the visit from her brother — "my dear good old queer brother with whom all my early happy days were spent." She knew that he had had a hard life in America. After her last visit to him in Monroe, "I was very much out of spirits when I returned here, thinking how hard you are obliged to work, and that I could do nothing for you, but on reflection I feel comforted by the thought that if you are not rich, you are respected, and if your *hands* are so hard your *heart* is yet tender & in the right place, a pretty rough looking customer you are got to be my dear brother, and yet I felt quite satisfied to ride in your old waggon, and bawl into your deaf ear . . . I hope yet to see you as you used to be in the 'olden time'."

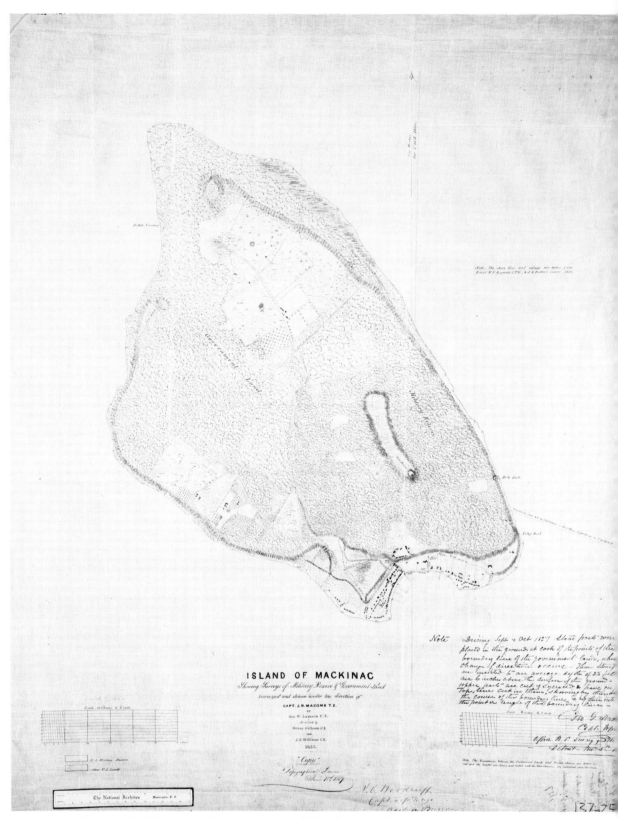

Captain J. M. Macomb's 1853 map of Mackinac Island

His farming must have gone a little better since then, for now that he was coming to Mackinac she wrote in a postscript on the back of Lyster's letter: "If you can retain as many of those gold dollars you speak of as will hire a pair of horses now and then when you come up, you can bring a side saddle & I can renew the days of my youth once more. Allan says tell Uncle to bring Lightfoot, but Lyster gravely adds, 'oh no, don't Mama, for it would be quite too expensive.'"

No record remains of their horseback riding or the pigeon shooting, but it must have been a happy time. John Tull, as his brother-in-law said, was "a full souled fellow all sensibility and feeling, where he loves."

To see Lyster approaching manhood, engaging in manly activities and planning for a college education at West Point or elsewhere, brought both pride and sadness to his mother. When she wrote her customary birthday note to him to accompany his presents on his sixteenth birthday, she looked with anxiety into his future. "It may be the last birthday my Son that you will spend as a boy, beneath your parents' roof — and when you are gone from us, what a sorrowful day will it ever be to us, but we hope & look for great & good things from you dear Lyster, when you are gone out into the 'wide wide world' — of its evils you know nothing, of its excellences you may have formed an exaggerated estimate. Take with you my darling son into that world, your father's principles, his stern honesty, his thorough truthfulness, and above all, his religious faith, & you must & will do well."

The following summer was not all shooting and sport for Lyster. He took a job with Captain John Navarre Macomb of the topographical corps and tramped about the Island, not for pigeons, but with a surveying crew. His father was still enlisting the influence of friends to get him appointed to West Point or Annapolis, with no success whatever. It was decided that he would go in the fall of that year, 1853, to the University of Michigan. On October 20th he and his father went down to the harbor together and took a boat to Detroit. John accompanied him to Ann Arbor and turned him over to Professor and Mrs. G. Williams, in whose home he would live until the summer.

For Charlotte the parting had been pure misery. "I can scarcely believe that you left me only yesterday, so tediously have the hours dragged along, although I have had to employ every minute of them most sedulously, in order to finish the rest of your collars, &c, which I enclose, with two more shirts in the parcel . . . . I am continually thinking that I might have omitted something necessary to your comfort . . . I wish too, that I had gone down to the boat with you, but I felt that I could not do so with composure, nor could I say to you my darling boy one word of all that was pressing upon my heart. I could only pace up & down your little empty room, and entreat God to bless & protect you . . . oh! how I miss you my darling, at every step I turn to tell you something, & am checked by the sad thought that you are gone . . . Poor Bertie cried for half an hour because he did not see you before you left — and Allan & Noney mope about as if they were in search of something they cannot find."

All through the following winter the family's foremost concern was for letters from Lyster. "How many are our daily inquiries about the mail", his mother said; "it is our first thought in the morning, and to me really the *only* matter of interest." After the straits had frozen over in December, and no more boats could call, the Post Office had contracted with carriers to bring mail overland twice a month to Mackinac and the Sault. It was a long, hazardous journey through snow-filled forests and across the ice. Two mail carriers were lost that winter, Mackinac men, brother-in-law and son-in-law of Raveel, the blacksmith. Coming from the Sault, they were only a mile out from the Arched Rock when one froze to death and the other fell through the ice.

That winter was not quite as cold as usual — 16° below zero was the lowest reading on John's thermometer — but he thought it remarkably stormy and windy. His house, exposed on its hill, would shake and rock in the northwest winds until Charlotte was frightened. Major Williams, who had succeeded Major Larnard as Commandant, sent two masons in October to line the kitchen with lath and plaster, and John had puttered all about the house, sealing and stuffing chinks and cracks, but still it was cold and draughty. Instead of the usual firewood the Post was now supplying coal — a bad change, John thought, for the stoves were not adapted to it.

In addition to his other duties, he was teaching school this winter, instructing a few garrison children in a makeshift schoolroom in one of the buildings of the Fort. When he walked over there in the mornings the family dog, Caesar, would follow him, lie close to the schoolroom stove during class, go out with the children for recess, and hurry back to the stove again.

Lyster O'Brien — He was a 19 year old student at the University of Michigan when this ambrotype print was made in 1856. Until he went to the University his entire education had been by his parents. He had seen little of life except at Fort Mackinac, where he had lived since the age of five.

I remain.
    your affectionate son
        Lyster O'Brien.

When after long expectation letters from Lyster would finally arrive, there was great delight. "It was really amusing," John told Lyster, "to witness Bertie's joy at the receipt of your letter. He takes such care of the epistle (after his own fashion) that I fear there will be little of it in existence in a few days. After his mother read it, he crammed it into his pocket and flew down to Mary Baileys to read it. Poor little fellow, he shows so much feeling, that we love him more and more."

Mary Bailey — "our Mary" — was a warm and sympathetic young woman who had become Charlotte's best friend in the garrison. She was the daughter of the Post physician, Dr. Joseph Bailey, and lived with her parents in the Stone Quarters. Her younger brother, John Bailey, who was also at the University, studying medicine, did not write home as faithfully as Lyster did, so that sometimes Lyster's letters were his family's only information about him. The Baileys' neighbor in the Stone Quarters was the Commandant, Major Thomas Williams, an attractive, sensitive man, to whom Mary was engaged to be married.

In the spring of 1854 the break-up of the ice began earlier than usual. By April 21st boats were passing through the straits, such a line of sails in the first few days as John had never seen. A few

The Officers' Stone Quarters where the Commandant and the Post Physician lived.

Thomas Williams — Major Williams, a veteran of the Mexican War, was in command at Mackinac from 1852 to 1856. This photograph was taken about five years later, after he had been commissioned Brigadier General at the beginning of the Civil War. On August 5, 1862, he was killed in action at Baton Rouge.

miles from Mackinac a sidewheel steamboat, three "propellers" and several sailboats lay at anchor, awaiting a chance to come in through the zone of broken slabs of ice, pitching and heaving in the waves, that surrounded the Island. Charlotte was impatient to go; at the earliest opportunity, in the first week of May, she took a boat to Detroit to visit there and in Monroe and especially to see Lyster. Somewhat later John joined her; they did not return to Mackinac until June 6th, when they went up on the E. P. Collins. Lyster came home a few weeks later.

That summer the O'Briens had house guests again. The Rev. William Lyster, his wife and daughter, their old friends for whom their son was named, came to spend August with them. William Narcissus Lyster was, like John, an Irishman, and unlike John, an enthusiastic poet. Some of his recent poems, he proudly stated, ran to a length of three hundred, even five hundred lines. His visit brought Charlotte the congenial treat of reading and talking poetry with a friend who shared her love for it.

Steamboat docks at Mackinac Island about 1871. Little had changed since the O'Brien's time.

The days grew shorter and cooler, and at the end of the month the Lysters departed. Aug. 31: "Dear Ellen, Mr. L. & Bessie left us — very autumnal weather." Charlotte had begun to keep a diary, brief pencil notes in a tiny booklet, "The Churchman's Diary 1854". She was feeling poorly as the autumn came on. On September 12th, her forty-second birthday, she "felt very ill all day". On the 13th and on the 14th she wrote simply "ill". Her friends were leaving as the summer declined. "Dear Kate left." — "Dear Mrs Bayley left." On the evening of the 18th "I had an attack of hemmorhage". Next day she was "better — but not suffered to move or speak". Not till the 22nd was she able to get up. She "Rode out with Lyster — very lovely warm day — & every thing appeared to me so beautiful — but feel very weak & old."

Sept. 23: "I sat up all day, & grew very tired, being so imprudent as to take a walk with L[yster]."

Sept. 24: "I had another hemorhage — everyone so very kind."

Sept. 27: "Another bleeding — all much alarmed & discouraged felt very ill & suffered unspeakably. Dearest M. watched." M. was her young friend Mary Bailey, who was Mrs. Williams now, having married the Major in early summer.

Sept. 29: "Better — most summerlike day — but all the glories of the fall pass by unnoticed by poor me."

On October 1st and 2nd there were hemorhages from the lungs again: "Another dreadful bleeding — suffered greatly from a sense of suffocation — reduced to great weakness."

Weak as she was, she was helping to get Lyster's clothes ready for his return to the University, when suddenly he was seized by a violent illness. This seemed too much to bear. "Help us oh Lord our God", she wrote in the diary. Lyster presently recovered and waited for a boat. Reports of shipping disasters were coming in.

Oct. 12: "News of the loss of the E. P. Collins — oh how terrible." She and John had returned on the Collins in June.

Oct. 13: "*No boat* for below that L. could travel on — besides he is not quite well yet — dreadful news of the loss of the steamship Artic with 400 souls on board." One of them, she learned later, was her good friend Mrs. Scott.

Oct. 14: "No boat. dearest Mary & the Major left in the horrid Sultana ... May the Lord preserve my darling Mary." Either the Sultana was too horrid or her destination was not Detroit, for Lyster did not go with Mary and the Major. But a suitable boat called the next day, and then he departed.

Charlotte had decided that she herself must go to Detroit for medical help. She had no confidence in Dr. Bailey. Her own John, she thought, was a far better physician than he. Her trunk was packed and she was ready for the trip, but she hesitated.

Oct. 17: "Suppose I shall go by the Elgin — fear J[ohn] will not go, which is a great trial to me. better today thank God."

Oct. 22: "Suppose I go tomorrow by the Troy, but dear J. seems opposed to it. very much disturbed & perplexed not knowing what to do."

Oct. 23: "Decided not to go today. I think dear J is pleased at it. wrote to dear L[yster] & Mary — how I *do* miss that dear child."

Oct. 24: "Feel rather more quiet & easy — perhaps it w^d be better to give up all idea of leaving home — whatever happens, may I be resigned & thankful."

Oct. 25: "Michigan came today, when we did not expect her till tomorrow — J asked me if we should go — I said no — hope it will prove for the best."

Oct. 26: "So lovely that had the boat come this morning, we shd certainly have gone. May the Lord guide us."

Oct 27: "No boat — No boat."

Oct 30: "Finally decided that I shall not leave the Island. hope to feel contented, & that please God my health may be restored ... May I have patience and grace to bear all things."

Nov. 2: "Summoned courage to unpack my trunk."

At this time Dr. Bailey departed and was replaced by Dr. Brown, the same physician who had treated Mrs. Larnard's last illness — and misjudged it. John O'Brien was greatly cheered, for he thought highly of Dr. Brown.

To hindsight from a later time it seems very plain that Charlotte had pulmonary tuberculosis — night fevers, a cough, shortness of breath, the hemorhages — but neither Dr. Bailey nor Dr. Brown seems to have diagnosed it as such. Dr. Brown "has never supposed that her lungs were diseased — he found her in a debilitated state and to restore her from that has been the difficulty." Perhaps it made little difference whether the disease was recognized or not. There was no cure for consumption in those days, no more in Detroit than at Mackinac. Dr. Brown treated symptoms; he prescribed cough medicines; when one type deranged her digestion, he would change to another. She as well as John "entertained the highest opinion of Dr. Brown and his care and assiduity and skill in meeting the verious symptoms." Sore throat, sore mouth, skin rash, headache, fever — he treated them all as her illness continued through the slow months of oncoming winter. She would feel a little better or a little worse. She was "too peevish and troubled about many things." She was annoyed by her servant and sometimes by her children too. "Very nervous — dear Allan's carelessness affects me too much — how I need grace and patience."

Confined to the house, she was lonely. The summer people were leaving. "Mrs. Reynolds came to bid me goodbye ... Mrs. Irvine to bid adieu — feel very sad as one after another leaves us." Friendships, affections, visiting, meeting, talking: these were the very substance of her life; but now "I feel as if my island friends imagine I have some infectious complaint, so few do I see." And

72

Letter by John O'Brien dated April 24, 1854. This is the first use of a postage stamp on any of the O'Brien letters.

again: "How seldom do my friends (so called) come to see me — almost all who really loved me are gone."

Worst blow of all, "Major W[illiams] returned but alas! without Mary — so told my fears — & now I must make up my mind for a most lonely winter . . . feel very very sad & heartsick." Mary had stayed with her parents at Fort Hamilton where Dr. Bailey was then stationed. This must have been for family reasons or to avoid the bitter Mackinac winter and not because there was any trouble in her marriage. Poor Major Williams was "so sad & woebegone."

Though he still lived "below", he took his meals with another officer's family next door in the Hill Quarters. Charlotte was glad of this, for so she saw him often and he spent many evenings with her and John.

For John of course the months of Charlotte's illness had been anxious and hard. He took care of her and waited on her, and when she had headache or other suffering in the night he sat up with her, until he too seemed to her to be ill with fatigue. "Dear J. quite poorly — he looks sick — am glad he has not to go out." He assumed much of the burden of housekeeping and, as he told Lyster, "acquired during your dear mother's illness some skill in culinary operations." All this he undertook with patience and good will. He even made somewhat labored jokes of the difficulties that arose. In December the ice closed off navigation before the usual winter supplies had been brought in, so that the Island was "deprived of certain comforts always deemed indispensable, viz fresh butter eggs & fresh pork . . . I want to persuade your dear mother and the boys, that sausages are undigestible and therefore not suitable food. They view this a new theory & are not yet reconciled to it. I cannot persuade them that on a very cold morning that sausages and buck wheat cakes are not suitable for breakfast."

December 7th was Lyster's birthday, and Charlotte cried in speaking of him. Her thoughts seemed to focus on him more and more. When she was able to do nothing else, she wrote to him, and when his letters came they lifted her spirits. Through that month of December her health seemed to be improving. On the 16th she was "Better towards night than I have ever yet been — for which I desire to be deeply thankful — mail — nice letter from L." On the 18th "rather better altogether today — only wish my spirits & my nerves were in better order." On Christmas day Major Williams came to have dinner with the O'Briens. Next morning Charlotte was pleased to find herself "Much less tired than I expected — feel also quite contented & in better spirits than usual." She felt so well indeed that on the 27th "J. & I went & pd the Major quite a visit it being a most lovely day — windows open & bright sun." On that happy note the diary ended.

John was encouraged by the intermission of Charlotte's disease. He still regarded the course of her illness as a long slow recovery rather than an irregular decline. To him she seemed better in December than she had been in October. Dr. Brown endorsed this point of view, saying that his patient was "getting on as well as could be expected." John thought she would recover sooner if she would rest more and not trouble herself so much with household matters. He himself was easy-going and good-humored about disorder or confusion in the house, and he wished that she would just let things go along in their own way. That she could not do. Her home and her family were the work of her life, and they had to be just right.

The hopeful mood in which the year ended was reflected in one of John's letters to Lyster: "I am glad to say that your dear Mother is improving in health, & by the blessing of God will be restored to her usual state. Quiet she needs, but her habits have been heretofore too active & industrious to remain as still as she ought. The boys are not the tidiest urchins in existence, and hence when your mother leaves her room and comes into the parlour and little study, she sees with the eyes of Argus a shoe here a stocking there a cap a coat hats gloves and pants in fact instead of finding a place for every thing and every thing in its place, I fancy she supposes every thing is out of place — then Allan Noel come here take away this, put up that — O Bertie what is this — John here is a dozen of articles belonging to you — why I thought I put them all out of the way. Then comes in Master Caesar covered with snow and leaving the print of his broad paws behind him — call Mary to sweep away the snow, turn the dog out, and by this time Caesar has his paws and nose close to the stove. Mary appears with the broom & attempts to dislodge the poor animal, he yields no obedience to the hired servant, thinks himself insulted and ill used. He shows his indignation by a growl. Mary strikes him with the broom, he rouses himself snarls & barks, away she goes in a fright, tells the mistress what a wicked dog that Saysar is, to the no small amusement of the boys."

So the family's life went on contentedly in its everyday course, and a veil of hope blurred reality for John. But in February, writing to Lyster, he had to admit that "Your dear Mother is not as well as we could wish." He added at once that she was by no means so ill as she had been when Lyster last saw her. He surely felt more anxiety than he showed, for she was running a fever at night and her pulse was usually over 100. Dr. Brown had begun to fear "that some insidious disease of the lungs was going on, but nothing to apprehend immediate danger from." The danger, however, was very immediate, for her death was only a few weeks away. Though she spent her days in bed, she continued to get up every evening and join her family in the parlor for a few hours. Presently even that was impossible, and on March 12th she took a severe turn for the worse and her strength failed. Dr. Brown, abandoning all hope, began to give her opiates to mitigate her pain in her last few days. For much of the time she lay in a drugged half-slumber. Whether asleep or awake she kept speaking of Lyster and whether the mail had come. She knew now that she was dying. On March 16th she spoke about arrangements for her funeral. "They tell me my situation is critical", she said to a friend who was with her. "I may live but if I die may the Lord forgive me all my sins and receive me to himself."

Just how things happened on the day of her death, the 17th, was never clear in John's mind, so stunned was he. "During morning prayer we are in the habit of singing on this morning I think I brought my three little boys into her bedroom who sat on a sofa & commenced Rock of Ages my dear wife said too low or higher and Allan tells me he raised the hymn a little higher." A Mrs. Culbertson, in attendance, thought that Mrs. O'Brien, unable to sing, hummed the tune. John read from the Book of Isaiah. He asked Charlotte whether she could understand. She answered "The spirit is willing but the flesh is weak." Later, about noon, he brought his weeping children into the bedroom again. He read from Corinthians and then read Bishop Andrews' litany, concluding with "Christ that redeemed thee with his agony and bloody death have mercy upon thee ... Amen. Christ that rose the third day from the dead, raise up thy body again at the resurrection of the just. Amen ... God the father preserve and keep thee. God the son assist & strengthen thee. God the Holy Spirit defend & aid thee. God the Holy Trinity be ever with thee, that thy death may be precious in the sight of the Lord, with whom thou shalt live for evermore. Amen. These I believe were the last words the dear loved one heard on this side eternity."

Allan said that she died very calmly with a smile upon her face and did not appear to suffer much.

In a sense, she had set down her own last words long ago in the Covenant she had made with God when she was seventeen: "Oh Lord, when thou seest the agonies of dissolving nature upon me ... Look down, Oh my Heavenly Father, with a pitying eye upon thy languishing dying child; put strength and confidence into my departing spirit, and receive it to the embraces of thy everlasting love."

Charlotte's grave

Eliza Cooper on the Isle of Wight heard promptly from John Tull of his sister's death. During all the years of separation Eliza had continued to write to her beloved friend, to send English newspapers and boxes of gifts. She regarded herself as a member of the family. To the O'Brien boys, whom she had never met, she was their loving Aunt Eliza. When Lyster went to college, she undertook to send ten pounds toward his expenses.

After she had heard the dreadful news, she waited, confidently expecting a letter from John O'Brien about her adored friend's last days and hours. None came. "Weeks passed by, at length they amounted to months. I cannot tell all the disappointment I experienced. Dear Charlotte's husband and children I had loved for her sake, and felt myself treated as a stranger, as one who had no interest in them . . . And when at last after the lapse of many months a letter came, the formal 'Dear Madam' chilled me to the very heart . . . freezing coldness and stranger-like indifference pervaded it."

She sent the ten pounds promised for Lyster, and she upbraided John for his neglect and chilliness. "If I have judged you harshly, forgive me. Warm hearted myself, . . . I perhaps expect too much from others. Had I loved dear Charlotte less I had felt less keenly. She was the only being I ever cared to call my friend, indeed, I looked on her as a sister and my love for her was a sister's love."

Poor John, wrapped in his own grief, had doubtless written in a distant, formal way that deserved her chiding letter. Perhaps he couldn't help it. It was his nature. His manner had always been stiff, reserved, ponderous. After Charlotte died, some light within him had died also. Indeed she had been the joy, the vitality, the warmth of his being; she was his guide in the world of everyday human affairs and affections. She had been his heart. After she was gone, he seemed to withdraw into his study, into an intellectual existence with his books and papers, his sermons, his Bible.

The O'Brien boys carried on as well as they could, clinging to the Christian consolations that their parents had earnestly taught them. They all felt as Allan did: "Truly this is the first time in fifteen years that I have known what real affliction is."

When John, making his usual June expedition to Detroit, took Bertie with him, Allan was considered old and responsible enough to be left in charge at home with Nony. He wrote to his father, "we were very glad to hear that you had a pleasant passage down for it was very stormy here. We have finished cleaning house and did not have much trouble except about the white washing however we got that done at last and then the worst part was over . . . I suppose Bertie would like to be at home again, though our home is not what it once was while my dear Mother was living. May the Lord give us patience to submit to this our sad bereavement with becoming resignation and instead of thinking and feeling how dark and gloomy every thing is without her, let all of us look forward

with joy to the time when we made pure through the blood of Jesus Christ shall be with her for ever and ever."

In some ways Allan seemed the most promising of the O'Brien boys. He was manly, likeable, affectionate, and perhaps more mature at age fifteen than Lyster had been. It was a wanton tragedy when in July a sudden illness felled him — no one knew what it was — and he died four months after his mother. They buried him beside her. One face of the marble obelisk bears his name.

The other boys lived long lives, well into the 20th century. After Lyster graduated from the University in 1858, he studied law in Detroit until his father accumulated enough money to send him to Harvard Law School. "I have done all in my power to give you the benefit of the best education this state affords," his father told him, and "I wished you to have the advantage of the best legal institution in the Union." Lyster was admitted to the bar in Detroit; but before he was well started in practice, the expanding Civil War disrupted their lives. Lyster helped to organize a company in the 27th Michigan Volunteer Infantry, in which he was commissioned a Second Lieutenant. John meanwhile had lost his Chaplaincy when the troops were withdrawn from Fort Mackinac in 1861. After some difficulty he obtained a parish in Pontiac, Zion Episcopal Church, where he remained until his sudden death by a stroke in December, 1864.

Lyster's was one of twenty Union regiments that took the heaviest losses; he himself was wounded before Petersburg. After the war he had no heart for a civilian career; a child of Fort Mackinac, the military life was in his blood; he reenlisted in the regular army and served for thirty-five years, through Indian campaigns and through the Spanish War, until his final retirement in 1901 with the rank of Colonel.

Neither Nony nor Bertie received any education except their father's teaching, for he simply could not afford to send them to college. He kept them close to him during the war. His control over them was strong, and he restrained them from enlisting. Instead he helped them to get jobs. After his death they became prosperous business men in Detroit, Noel a broker and banker, Herbert with a pharmaceutical company. Every summer of their lives, it was said, they used to return to Mackinac and would walk, carrying flowers, up that woodland road where once on a bitter March day they had walked in a snowstorm. When they came to the cemetery they would stand again by their mother's grave and lay their flowers upon it.

Letter written by Charlotte O'Brien on August 16, 1846. The creases show how it was folded for mailing. On two of the flaps that were folded under is a dictated message from Lyster to Allan, on the third a postscript by Charlotte. Marks of the sealing wax remain. Many of the O'Brien letters were mailed in this manner.

From boyhood Edward Nicholas has been fascinated by history and biography. History was his major field at Princeton and in graduate study at Harvard and at Cambridge, England. Since then his activities have been manifold. In Columbus, Ohio, where he was born in 1906, he is well known as a business man, manager of downtown properties. In New Mexico he operated a cattle ranch and an irrigated farm. Meanwhile he wrote a book, *The Hours and the Ages,* a biographical interpretation of American history, published in 1949. He still visits Columbus often but resides mainly in Santa Fe. There he continues to follow his historical bent, serving on the managerial boards of the Archaeological Conservancy and the School of American Research.

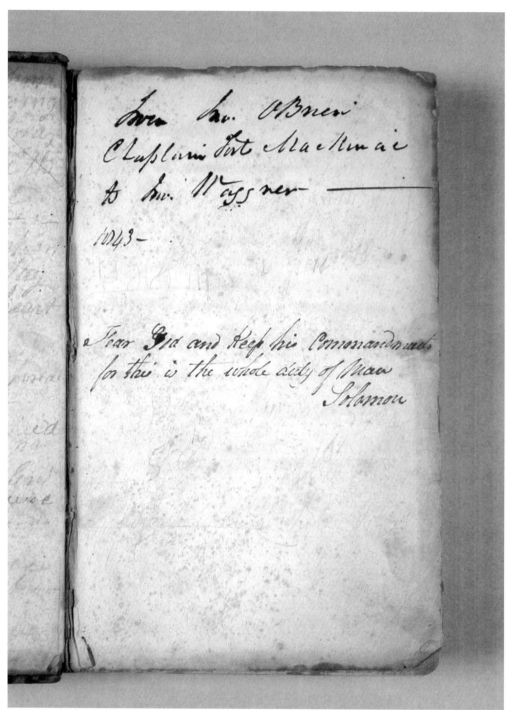

Reverend John O'Brien presented this Bible to First Sergeant John H. Waggner at Fort Mackinac in 1843. The 34-year-old Waggner arrived at Fort Mackinac with Company "I", 5th Regiment of Infantry on November 6, 1841. He served at the fort until the end of his enlistment three years later. Waggner was a staunch supporter of the Confederacy during the Civil War and chronicled his pro-southern opinions in his Bible. The Bible, acquired in 1999, is a rare find and one of the few objects in Mackinac State Historic Parks' collection that was owned and used by a Fort Mackinac soldier.